.wealth

.wealth

Value Creation and Capture in the Digital Economy

Stefan H. Nguyen

Published by Next Ignite, Inc.

12707 High Bluff Dr., Ste. 200, San Diego, CA 92130

http://nextignite.com

Phone 858.242.2823 • Fax 858.794.1450

First Printing: November 2011

ISBN: 0615562884
ISBN-13: 978-0615562889

To My Grandmother,

Who taught me the greatness of sacrifice…

To My Mother and Father,

The two greatest persons I know.

Table of Contents

"Once a new technology rolls over you,
if you're not part of the steamroller,
you're part of the road."

-Stewart Brand

Introduction

Now is a new era for business. Global markets, global customers, and global access have brought into effect the laws of large numbers, of mass customization, of giant, interconnected networks, social and otherwise. Internet companies have begun to prove that they can achieve revenue and amass profits. The social networks such as Facebook, Meetup, and LinkedIn have themselves connected with each other. Multiple touch-points now exist among businesses and their customers, suppliers, partners, and even competitors. Channels continue to increase and evolve. A website is just a starting point for digital presence. Businesses must also make themselves known on Twitter, Facebook, LinkedIn, YouTube, tablets, and smart phones - to name only a few.

Business has become more than just developing a good product, shepherding it to market, and closing sales. The connected economy demands an awareness of customers' lifetime values and a view of the overall interactions of numerous participants in the company's business network, with its multitude of interactions and values. From customers providing instant recognition and ratings for the venues they visit, to partners sending referrals and expecting reciprocity, businesses need to be responsive and agile, forward-thinking, and inventive. They must be technologically savvy and accountable, digitally and otherwise, to better manage reputation, enhance partnerships, and complete the loops of engagement. The gaps between consumers and providers continue to close. Overlaps continue to increase along the supply chain and the sales channels, especially when it comes to information signals, awareness, and coordination.

The spectacular and, at times, overwhelming valuations of some digital companies, justified or not, do offer us a glimpse into the future of business.[1] It is about numerous exchanges of values. It is also about the aggregation of values that, in individual pieces seem infinitesimal, yet, in large numbers, become significant, and even disruptive. A dozen years ago, we wondered how a click on a link is worth money to some

---

[1] **Kelly, Kate.** Facebook IPO Valuation Could Top $100 Billion: Sources. *CNBC.* [Online] 06 13, 2011. http://www.cnbc.com/id/43378490.

company somewhere. We wondered how Hotmail could afford to give out free email accounts in the millions when some of us are paying $20 a month for email service. Was Google just a bunch of all-around computer-savvy philanthropists wanting to help the world look for information on the Internet? How can LinkedIn afford to let tens of millions use its service without ever paying a dime, relegating the rolodex to the museum?

These new economy darlings represent a new kind of entity, businesses that are virtual, seemingly simple, yet incredibly intricate, with unheard-of agility. They are teeming with numbers, measures, statistics, and, most importantly, interconnections that drive their value propositions, and perhaps their very existence. And one can learn a lot from them.

The digital landscape has forever been superimposed onto business. Digital capabilities are a must-have to compete. Digital transformation has disrupted multiple industries from newspapers to movie rentals to advertising. Whether one's goal is to create the next Facebook or to simply transform one's professional practice to better compete in the digital age, it is critical to understand and emulate the make-up of a new business entity that is digitally leveraged, interconnected, highly adaptable, nimble, and incredibly efficient. Moreover, it is one based on a resilient and sustainable network.

What are some of the characteristics of this network?

- It involves multiple individuals and organizations that gather as different types of participants.

- Within the network, there are numerous interactions at multiple levels, achieving a critical state of density and liquidity.

- There are also numerous and multi-instance transactions, of exchanges for different kinds of values, be it money, recommendations, contacts, advice, or just random conversations.

- Sustainability of the network is dependent on the overall numbers, not individual interactions.

Does this network represent a market? Does it represent an economy? Based on the textbook definition of a market and the extent of a market, it can be considered a system of multiple markets, but not an economy. This network most closely resembles what economists term an "n-sided market."

James F. Moore first used the term "business ecosystem" to describe this type of networks.[2] For reasons that will be clear in subsequent discussions of this book, we use the term "capital ecosystem" as we are interested in exchanges of values beyond financial. We aim to demonstrate the power of capital ecosystems in the digital domain to create and capture overwhelming wealth. Our goal is to provide entrepreneurs, business executives, and even non-profit organizers, a way of thinking, and an effective framework, to unlock the digital genie that can recognize, stimulate, capture, and shape the enormous values coursing through our evermore connected world.

---

[2] **Moore, James F.** Predators and Prey: A New Ecology of Competition. *Harvard Business Review.* May/June 1993.

Chapter

1

> "When one tugs at a single thing
> in nature, he finds it attached to
> the rest of the world."
>
> -John Muir

1. Capital Ecosystems

*W*ebster's defines an ecosystem as "a system formed by the interaction of a community of organisms with its environment." Iansiti and Levien, in their book *The Keystone Advantage,* provided further conceptualization of Moore's "business ecosystem" and the "ecosystem strategy".[3] The digital era's quickening pace of global business and interconnectedness continues to demonstrate the concept. It is time to think of the business as more than just an entity in itself, more than just its self-interests. The age of partnership has started and matured. Co-opetition is a viable business strategy.[4] If we haven't done so, it is time for us to look at business in the context of the

---

[3] **Iansiti, Marco and Levien, Roy.** *The Keystone Advantage: What the New Dynamics of Business Ecosystems Mean for Strategy, Innovation, and Sustainability.* Boston : Harvard Business School Publishing, 2004.

[4] **Brandenburger, Adam M and Nalebuff, Barry J.** *Co-Opetition.* New York : Currency Doubleday, 1996.

ecosystem in which it exists and operates. We introduce the concept of "capital ecosystems" to recognize both financial and non-financial capitals that are exchanged within a business network. The capital ecosystem accounts for the way an enterprise conducts its business with partners, customers, suppliers, regulators, competitors, community, and the public within a network in which information and a multitude of values are exchanged effectively among participants.

The "ecosystem" metaphor is valuable for multiple reasons. When the view of values and interests is enlarged beyond the boundaries of the business, a better understanding of value creation emerges. More realistic accounting for the business's need of, use of, and responsibility for public goods ensues. Problems and conundrums that occur in the individual context have a better chance of being solved in the larger context, made possible by the existence of additional types of values, channels of communications, and value exchanges.

Seeing a business within its capital ecosystem allows one to appreciate the necessary investments to create fair and lasting value, to innovate beyond the business's borders and incorporate innovations in technology, processes, and practices that constantly arise - with or without its intervention

- to better understand and respond to its customers, suppliers, regulators, partners, and competitors. Organizations do not want to miss out on the information exchanges and market signals that bypass so many incumbents and ultimately foreshadow their demise.

The capital ecosystem borrows its concepts of sustainability from the commonly understood ecosystem paradigm. Sustainability, alignment, and optimization of the ecosystem's values mean overall wealth creation for its members. Participants in the ecosystem win when overall value is created in the network, and they are rewarded with the accumulation of capitals, and wealth, earned through their exchanges with other members of the network.

The key cost of operating and participating in a capital ecosystem has been the required coordination. In many instances, especially in the past, this cost has proved prohibitive. With the advent of technology for communication, transactions, and collaboration, this cost has decreased dramatically. Witness the emergence of the virtual corporation.[5] Now is the time to view a business beyond its

---

[5] **Davidow, William H and Malone, Michael S.** *The Virtual Corporation.* New York : Harper Business, 1992.

corporate walls, to extend understanding, strategy, planning, investments, decisions, and execution to the capital ecosystem, where enormous opportunities and value await.

The value potential of a system can be measured by its span, density, value exchanges, and value capture. In the chapters that follow, we define these measures and apply them to the capital ecosystem, paying special attention to the digital platforms that are an intricate part of this wonder of a network, in the same way that an environment serves its ecosystem. These platforms enable the interaction and value exchange, capture, aggregation, transformation that fuel capital accumulation and wealth within the capital ecosystem.

Value Potential in a Network

We present that the goal of a capital ecosystem is to create value for the overall system. Value creation requires interaction and value exchange. Sustainable value exchange requires a density of interacting units. When the interactions produce values in alignment, so that they amplify the values and the effects of those values, efficiency is further achieved. Additionally, when instances of the same values can be accumulated, the aggregated value becomes significant due to the large number of value-creating interactions from the dense network. It is difficult to argue how one web surfer glancing at an ad on the right sidebar of a Google search result page can be worth anything. Yet, as we now know, billions of dollars are made by Google each quarter from the collective glances of Internet users through its AdWords.[6]

The potential value, or wealth, creation within a network can be judged by its:

- Span

- Connections

- Density

- Interactions

- Value exchanges

- Value capture

- Value alignment

- Value aggregation

- Value transformation efficiency

---

[6] **Google, Inc.** Summary of Google, Inc. - Yahoo! Finance. *Yahoo! Finance.* [Online] May 10, 2011. http://biz.yahoo.com/e/110510/goog10-q.html.

These measures represent the metrics required not only for the sustainability of a network, but also that network's potential for value creation and disruptive powers.

Common descriptions of networks tend to highlight the number of members. However, that is only one, and perhaps the most superficial, measure. Beyond member count, there is the span of the network, or how far it reaches given its members, and how diverse and influential its members are. Span points to the potential of the network to achieve a great number of connections. The more connections there are in a network, the higher that network's density. Without critical density, there may not be adequate interactions and value exchanges occurring to create meaningful values for all participants involved. One can take the simplest case where a network of only two parties formed for the exchange of goods and/or services for money. This is the classic definition of a transaction. The by-products of one transaction, such as information, purchase behavior, customer service, and discount, may not be significant to be of any value to a third party. However, as we can see in the case of Groupon, the aggregated values of thousands of transactions can create enormous returns for all parties involved, such that everyone feels that he or she received "a good deal".[7]

If the simple goals of a business model are to create and capture wealth, then wealth is created through interactions and exchanges in the same way that energy is released when certain chemicals interact. This principle has been the basis for engines, ranging from the simple carburetors to rocket launchers. Energy can be released with a trigger, e.g., gas lit with a spark, nuclear fusion achieved with a concentrated beam of laser. Uncontrolled, the explosions can have disastrous consequences. Controlled, enormous power can be harnessed and channeled.

By the same token, interactions and value exchanges within a capital ecosystem can be created with catalysts. Catalysts can be as simple and well-understood as marketplaces, user conferences, or meetings. They can be as complex and virtual as options or futures contracts on an exchange.

Values created from interactions must be captured. As the reader will recognize in the chapters that follow, enormous wealth can be created by the recognition of new values and the

---

[7] **Steiner, Christopher.** Meet The Fastest Growing Company Ever. *Forbes Magazine.* August 30, 2010, p. 3.

design of a system or systems to capture, aggregate, and transform them.

Values created from interactions must also be aligned across interactions and within interactions to amplify and add to the aggregate values. Misalignment resulting from disinformation, disincentives, mistrust, or conflicting signals can weaken or altogether do away with any values created. That is, without alignment, values can uncontrollably negate or deemphasize each other.

Value aggregation is important when values created exist in such minute and insignificant amounts that they must be channeled, captured, collected, and aggregated into something significant.

Aggregation of values is also important for value transformation. Some values, without critical minimal aggregation, cannot be converted to other required values. For example, without enough traffic through a website for CPM (cost per thousand impressions), transformation of site visits to advertising revenue cannot be achieved.[8]

---

[8] **Chaffey, Dave, et al., et al.** *Internet Marketing: Strategy, Implementation, Practice.* Essex : Pearson Education Limited, 2009.

Re-inventing the business so that it is firmly supported by a sustainable capital ecosystem with high value creation potential is a must in the new economy. The bonus from this re-invention is that the very same capital ecosystem will organically provide high barriers to entry, as we shall see in the coming chapters.

Chapter

2

> "Wealth, like happiness, is never attained when sought after directly. It comes as a by-product of providing a useful service."
>
> -Henry Ford

2. The Digital Wealth Engine

W e begin our exploration of the engine that creates digital wealth with the examination not so much of the gears and the shafts, but of the soft matter that is so critical to the direction, control, and restraint of the machine. If a vehicle is the metaphor for a value-creating capital ecosystem, and horsepower is the metaphor for its value potential, then the states to which the ecosystem can transition are the various target destinations. Together the set of states or milestones that are suitably planned and reached provide the roadmap to sustainability and optimality for the ecosystem. We begin with a discussion of how this roadmap is formulated and implemented as navigation for our value vehicle.

The Soft Stuff

As any business person can tell us, business is more than just theory, numbers, diagrams, and supply/demand curves. It is about evangelizing, selling, follow-up, service renewals, and, more and more significantly - reputation. It is easy to see how value is created with tangible tasks such as order taking, shipping, and payment deposits. It is harder to identify intangibles such as reputation, customer loyalty, public trust, and partner commitment.

Expectations and Trust

We normally afford those around us a certain level of trust. Watching a movie, we happily engage in the suspension of disbelief, trusting the filmmaker to deliver entertainment with the rope that we've given him. Every business proposition requires trust. When we buy products online, we trust that our credit card information will not be stolen, and we trust that the shipment will reach our home properly and without damage. The latest snafus of customer information being stolen and accessed at large corporations such as Sony[9] and Citicorp[10]

---

[9] **Associated Press.** Sony says 25 million more accounts hacked. *USA Today.* May 3, 2011, p. 1.

[10] **Reuters.** Thousands of Citi customers at risk after hacker attack. *Thompson Reuters.* 2011.

continually highlight the criticality of security to online commerce. Our expectations of certain performance reliability are reciprocal to this trust. As expectations are met by the vendor, our trust is solidified, and the vendor is rewarded with a good reputation. Relationships then evolved to higher levels of trust and approach loyalty. If expectations are not met, trust evaporates, and reputations suffer.

Snake Oil Salesmen and Visionaries

What distinguishes industry visionaries from snake oil salesmen? It is in the delivery of the vision versus the lack of proof for the outrageous claims. Trust is built as claims are backed up by delivery. Of course, many captains of industry have chosen to speak with their products rather than their mouths before any items are delivered. However, most inventions require evangelizing and galvanizing of efforts, if only within the founding team or the product development environment, as support and contributions of multiple groups and individuals are needed. As any entrepreneur can attest, the elevator pitch is important to achieving the interest of the venture capital community, but then a fully flushed out strategy and a believable plan must be presented. Even after an investment is made, measures and metrics are kept to ensure performance is as planned before additional portions of promised funding are delivered.

Why Vision Matters

Because every business transaction is a proposition, every business plan is a hypothesis, until its value creation is proven. Even then, as we learn from the scientific method, it is just a theory, not a law, and it is correct only until proven otherwise. We suspend our disbelief because we believe in the genius of the presenter before us, allowing him room to work his magic. This suspension gives our minds and our ideas the stretch that explores what can be, as opposed to what is. But make no mistake, we also constantly verify the logic of that exploration. The stretch is only for those degrees that bear sufficient probability. It is almost like an equation in which we vary one variable to see how the other variables respond and what final number we obtain. The variation of the variable that we allow, however, has constraints. Different integers can be substituted, but a haiku cannot be inserted, because then, the equation cannot be evaluated; that is, the variation does not logically follow from the patterns that we have been taught to evaluate an equation. Every business proposition is a reach, but that is how the envelope gets pushed and the mold gets broken. But there is always reciprocal expectation. That expectation has to be met, and meeting it requires execution and a commitment to sustain the business.

Execution and Commitment

Execution is the proof of the business proposition, a statement that what one suggested to the investors and the customers is an accurate forecast of the future. But most importantly, its goal is to satisfy the expectations of these stakeholders. Commitment reinforces trust and extends the proposition to the idea of sustainability of the business, but it is also reciprocated by expectations of continued business performance. Management then must be committed to satisfying the expectations of the shareholders.

The soft stuff matters most when a business plan is proposed and when a capital ecosystem is invented, because there are no hard numbers yet to empirically prove the execution. How should business propositions be constructed to be believable to attract support? How should they be constructed to be achievable in order to satisfy expectations, gaining trust of the stakeholders?

If the inspiration of a capital ecosystem is in its plan to gather and coordinate participants that optimally serve the system and individually benefit, the perspiration is the execution of the business events or transitions within the ecosystem to meet each participant's expectations. A CFO raises funds for a company, but also works to ensure the delivery of key financial metrics to meet expectations of the investors. A real estate agent brings together buyers and sellers, proposing a transaction that meets the needs of both parties, but his reputation is dependent on a deal that satisfies the expectations of both parties during and after the transaction.

Transitions and States

In business as in life, there are states that an entity traverses. The transition between states takes time, and some transitions have built-in delays, or latencies. Fortunately, in the digital universe, the transitions between states can occur very quickly, sometimes instantaneously, and without much coaxing. Natural transitions do occur and require little intervention.

Transitions that are planned and designed for particular purposes, such as when a start-up achieves its first sale, must be correctly calibrated to be realistic and attainable.

Transitions that are too abrupt risk being unachievable, as well as being unmanageable, with unforeseen, and sometimes disastrous, consequences.

Expectations and Implicit Contracts

Some transactions in markets occur with explicit legal contracts, but many occur based solely or partly on informal, implicit contacts. The ability to elicit explicit contracts that represent clearing expectations from both sides can catalyze transactions (i.e., transitions between states) and make markets. The options market is based on the clearing expectations of two parties about the probability of certain events.[11] A purchase of office equipment occurs as the equipment and currency change hands. The warranty on the equipment is based on an explicit contract of performance guaranteed by the manufacturer. However, the expectation of the service life of the equipment beyond the warranty period is based on the purchaser's assessment of the brand's quality and reliability.

The Groupon model discussed is based on the fulfillment of expectations from the both the consumers and the merchants.

---

[11] **McMillan, Lawrence G.** *Options as a Strategic Investment.* New York : Penguin Putnam, 2002.

The expectations set up implicit contracts that become explicit as certain criteria are met (e.g., 24-hour deal window, 100 total buyers for the deal). This model, first developed during the dotcom era of the late 1990's, has been copied by sites ranging from LivingSocial to local news' sites such as the San Diego Union Tribune's SignOnSanDiego Daily Deal.[12] For those who would like to go back even further, the model is a twist on the age-old loss-leader model, with the twist being the act of packaging the loss as gain for the consumers and taking it directly to them to secure pre-commitment.[13]

Another well-known example of an expectation market is KickStarter. Kickstarter substantiates the transition by providing transparency to the popularity of a proposed project, or state-of-play.[14] The expectation of a project's ability to secure a certain amount of funding within a specific timeframe, a proxy for its viability or popularity or both, engages the financial commitment of the supporters.

---

[12] **Mannes, Tanya.** Union-Tribune's Daily Deal hits big mark. *San Diego Union-Tribune.* April 22, 2011.

[13] **Surowiecki, James.** Groupon Clipping. *The New Yorker.* December 20, 2010.

[14] **Warren, Christina.** A Guide to Kickstarter & Crowd Funding [INFOGRAPHIC]. *Mashable.* [Online] January 17, 2011. [Cited: May 31, 2011.] http://mashable.com/2011/01/17/kickstarter-crowd-funding-infographic/.

Catalysts

Expectations and implicit contracts are types of catalysts. They not only serve to effect transactions, but also to keep transitions realistic, calibrated, and tractable. How? Catalysts that are implementable and executable, with effects or mutually fulfilled expectations that are identifiable, measurable, or can be experienced (e.g., 100 people agree to buy the $20 restaurant certificate for $10 by end of day tomorrow), usually result in realistic transitions. A key aspect of catalysts is that one catalyst can effect multiple transitions within a capital ecosystem.

Catalysts can be employed to achieve higher density, as when Hot or Not founders Hong and Young introduced the Meet Me feature to encourage adoption.[15] Catalysts can also be employed to effect interactions and exchanges, or to move from interactions to exchanges, as when groups organize networking events to exchange contacts or when startups pitch venture capitalists, online or offline. Catalysts can be employed to align values within an ecosystem when rules, structures, processes, and groups are organized around affinity.

---

[15] **Penenberg, Adam.** *Viral Loop.* New York : Hyperion, 2009.

Catalysts can even help aggregate value, as when search engine optimization (SEO) is employed to attract traffic to a site.

Catalysts can be defined broadly as any actions that can be employed on a capital ecosystem to bring about changes. They can be viewed as triggers, and can take the form of business events, technologies, processes, practices, or tasks. Catalysts may be actions taken by a business, but not every business action can serve as a catalyst. In other words, catalysts are meant to be effective in the context of an ecosystem, but not every business action yields an effect. Furthermore, an action can sometimes create unwanted or negative effects.

Businesses have over the years employed techniques that are essentially catalysts to increase density, stimulate interactions and exchanges, stoke customer demand, induce supply creation, and even create product scarcity. We will discuss some of these techniques while examining example businesses that are living proofs of well-designed capital ecosystems.

If our capital ecosystem is a vehicle, catalysts can serve as sparks that start the engine and let the machine hum to work progressing through different states of value creation and accumulation from network density to interactions, value exchanges, and value capture.

Value Projection

How does one devise the progression of states for an ecosystem that are achievable yet optimally quick? The secret does not lie in a theoretical master plan, but a series of planning and experimentation steps underscored by a keen and developing understanding of the participants and the ecosystem. This technique has been employed by countless online businesses that experiment with different business models, incentives, monetization schemes, and value creation activities. They range from the daily improvements made to Flickr by founders Caterina Fake and Stewart Butterfield[16] to the constant social media tweaks, advertising changes, and leveraging of volunteers that Markus Frind employs for PlentyOfFish.[17] The digital platform provides a medium for endless experimentation and observations of business strategies, tactics, and models. Biologists use fruit flies in their studies because the lifespan of fruit flies is extremely short. In his landmark book, *The Innovator's Dilemma*, HBS professor

---

[16] **Penenberg, Adam.** *Viral Loop.* New York : Hyperion, 2009.

[17] **Stross, Randall.** From 10 Hours a Week, $10 Million a Year . *The New York Times.* January 13, 2008.

Clayton Christensen referred to the disk drive companies as the fruit flies of business because of their short lifespans.[18] The lifespans of companies and business models in the Internet industry are similarly short. Many Internet companies and websites begin with "beta" versions just to experiment with their capital ecosystems and understand the dynamics of completely unknown markets that they are entering. A recent fascinating study by startup accelerator Blackbox (in collaboration with lean-startup guru Steve Blank) noted that startups which "pivot" their business or product one or two times raise 2.5 times more money.[19] The lean startup concept popularized by Steve Blank and Eric Reis advocates the quick and numerous build-measure-learn cycles that allow startups to calibrate themselves to a fast-moving or new market in which the novelty, attraction, and satisfaction of needs and desires of the consumers are not yet fully understood.[20]

Through series of experimentation and fact-gathering and with a deeper understanding of the relevant ecosystems, businesses can gain critical information about the participants, their

[18] **Christensen, Clayton M.** *The Innovator's Dilemma: The Revolutionary Book that Will Change the Way You Do Business.* New York : HarperCollins Publishers, 1997.

[19] **Marmer, Max, Herrmann, Bjoern Lasse and Berman, Ron.** Startup Genome Report. *Blackbox.* [Online] May 28, 2011. [Cited: May 31, 2011.] http://startupgenome.cc/pages/startup-genome-report-1.

[20] **Ries, Eric.** *The Lean Startup.* New York : Crown Business, 2011.

interactions, and their values. The process allows businesses to construct and refine ecosystems that are sustainable and resilient, though changing at breakneck speed. The process also includes numerous missteps that may or may not be detrimental to the business, but again, since these virtual businesses can so quickly start and end, the smart entrepreneurs take the lessons of even the failed efforts and utilized them in later successful attempts.

Our interest, however, is on the process by which the construction of appropriate states of transition for the ecosystem is carried out. The states must be designed in a series of steps that are based on the exchanges of values among the involved participants. The best states are those that create the most net values for the participants. However, beyond the net value gains in each state, the progression of states must be sustainable to allow the ecosystem to "grow" and "evolve" to a high-value state.

The set of values important to the participants and how the exchanges of these values can be triggered or catalyzed come from an understanding of the participant's value proposition - in the simplest sense, its business proposition. When the business propositions of multiple participants are connected and aligned in a series of value exchanges that make sense for all of them, a likely target state is identified. Then, once the overall value proposition to the participants can be established and catalysts are implemented to trigger them into interactions and value exchanges, a state transition will likely occur. Groupon establishes the overall value proposition to itself, the merchant, and the consumer by connecting the merchant's desire to sell at a certain quantity (to offset the proposed discount) to the consumer's desire to achieve a certain amount of discount, and then to its own desire for the exchange to occur.[21] The value proposition is clearly spelled out via the terms of the deal (e.g., expires or becomes real in 24 hours). Kickstarter provides the value proposition for financing by connecting crowds of potential investors to projects that expires after a certain period of time if funding goals are not met.[22]

In summary, the following key steps are taken to design a state for transition.

1. Assess what the participants need.

---

[21] **Dahlen, Christian.** Observations on Groupon Business Model - a Primer. *Slideshare.* [Online] November 2010. [Cited: May 31, 2011.] http://www.slideshare.net/dahlenc/groupon-business-model.

[22] **Warren, Christina.** A Guide to Kickstarter & Crowd Funding [INFOGRAPHIC]. *Mashable.* [Online] January 17, 2011. [Cited: May 31, 2011.] http://mashable.com/2011/01/17/kickstarter-crowd-funding-infographic/.

2. Design a "state of play" to satisfy their needs through realization of the reciprocal value exchanges.

3. Create a platform to catalyze - communicate "state of play", benefits, and likelihood via signals of reciprocal commitment. (Those interested in game theory might sense that this is a sort of foreshadowed variation on the solution to the prisoner-dilemma.)

The Hard Stuff

Proposition of states and catalysts for transitions gain commitment for the exchange of values in the capital ecosystem, but the system's span, density, connections, and interactions determine the likelihood of alignable value exchanges for state transitions. Also crucial to the net value gains are the actual value exchanges and the subsequent value capture, value aggregation, and value transformation.

We discuss below these elements as crucial components of a sustainability framework that will be shown to provide quantification to the capital ecosystem concept. Quantification will greatly improve both design and implementation of capital ecosystems and set the stage for performance measurement and monitoring.

Span

The span of a network is how far it reaches or spans given its nodes or members. Facebook significantly increases its span beyond the 800 million members (as of this writing) by introducing the Like feature. This feature allows the Facebook network to reach into far-flung corners of the Internet to any sites that its members enjoy, effectively allowing Facebook to incorporate other types of participants in its ecosystem. Span is more complicated to measure than member count. It also reflects the diversity of the member population, whether the diversity is enough for interactions and value exchanges to occur, and whether the diversity is too much and would cause misalignment in values and thereby disrupting interactions and value exchanges.

One way to assess span is through participant types. Different categorizations of participants can be employed. For example, participants can be classified at the highest levels as customers, suppliers, partners, etc., and at a more detailed level as first-time customers, repeat customers, referrals, etc. They can also be classified as influencers, early adopters, purveyors, etc. The number and types of classification should be moderated by the business's target span. Simply put, they should align with the business's target participants, whether they are customers, suppliers, or partners. Span is increased with additional members of the target groups, as well as additional groups that have been targeted.

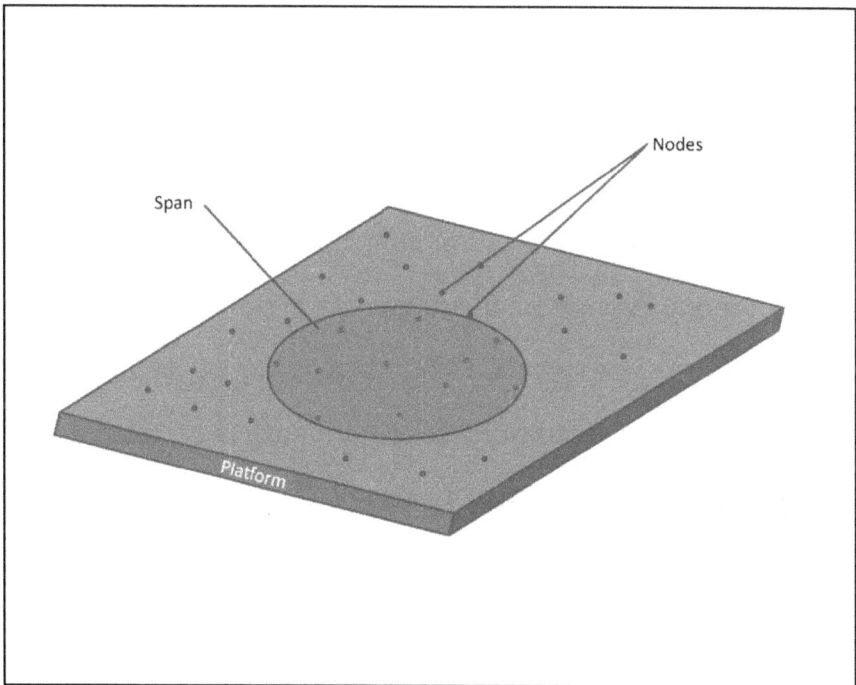

Figure 1 - The Span of a Network

Density

The density of a network is measured by the number of unique connections between nodes or sets of nodes. A network with 100,000 members that are unconnected to each other or are connected to only one leader has decent member count and possibly span, but perhaps not enough density. A network where only individual members can connect to each other has density, but only at one level. When groups of members can connect to other individual members or other groups of members, additional density is achieved. Email as a platform allows for connection among individual members, as well as among groups of members. It is no wonder that the email platform has spawned countless value exchanges, from simple newsletter communications to customer relationship management systems such as ConstantContact.[23]

---

[23] **ConstantContact.** Email Marketing Overview - Constant Contact. *Constant Contact.* [Online] May 31, 2011. [Cited: May 31, 2011.] http://www.constantcontact.com/email-marketing/index.jsp.

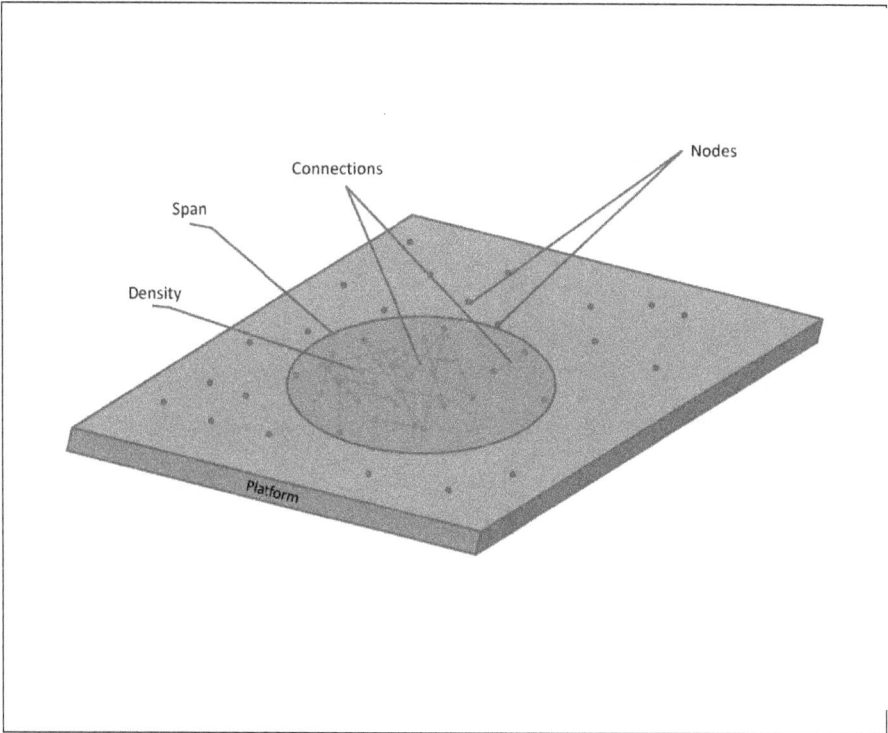

Figure 2 - Connections and Density

Interaction

The higher the density of a network, the higher the number of possible interactions, but connections alone are not sufficient for interactions. Connections exist for a reason, by design, affinity, or chance. Interactions can arise between connections to satisfy needs or to gain values. Interactions can be random exchange of meaningless conversations, or they can be highly valuable exchanges involving financial and intellectual capitals.

Catalysts, discussed earlier, are particularly useful for triggering interactions. They are responsible for step 2 in the sequence of state transition below:

1. Identify and validate desired state of play

2. Initiate the transition by:

    +   Removing barriers to interactions, and/or

    +   Provoking behaviors by:

        ▫   Communicating and/or substantiating the existence of the reciprocal behavior in the state of play

3. Complete the value flows

The discussion on states, contracts, and implicit expectations address step 1 above. Step 3 represents the tasks discussed below.

Value Exchange

All interactions involve some form of exchange. A conversation is an exchange of information. A sale is an exchange of a product or service for money. In a capital ecosystem, significant numbers of exchanges involve values other than money. In many cases, translated to their financial equivalents, the values involved could be worth enormous sums.

The more interactions that occur in a capital ecosystem, the more exchanges take place. The more and higher values that are exchanged, the higher the potential value created within the ecosystem.

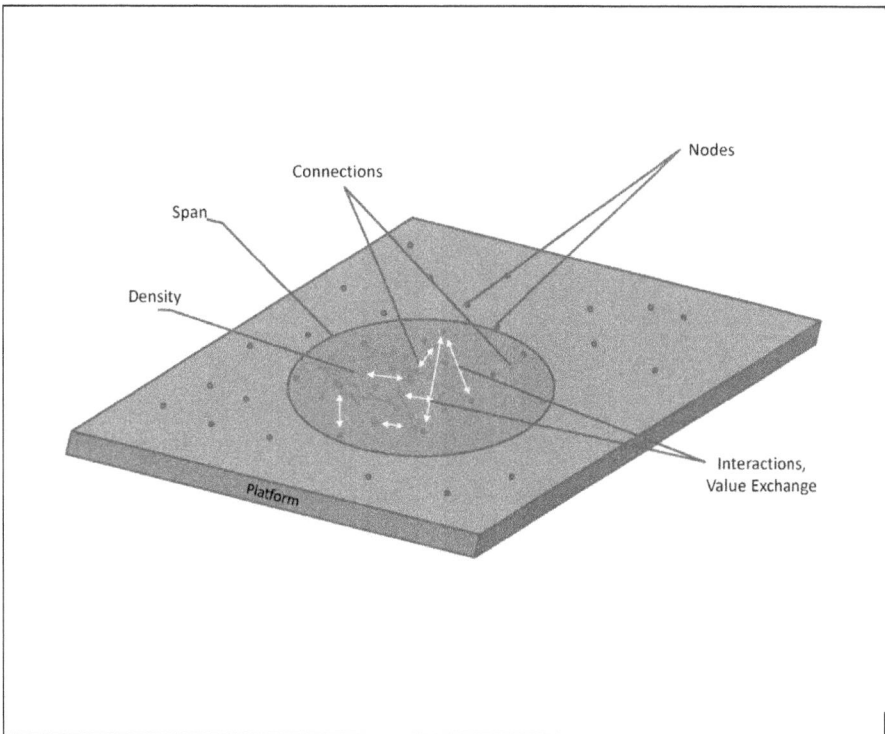

Figure 3 - Interactions and Value Exchange

Value Capture

Some values exchanged are difficult to capture. If a recommendation to a restaurant is made, the value of that information is captured by the receiver and the restaurant when the receiver visits the restaurant. However, the value of the appreciation expressed toward the referrer may not be possible to capture. On the web, referred-to destinations return the value to referrers by providing referral or affiliate commissions, in order to incentivize referrals. Offline, businesses attempt to close the loop with referral rewards. Apartment renters and human resources departments have practiced this technique for years. A recent example is DIRECTV's referral bonus of $100 for each friend that its subscribers refer.[24]

Within a capital ecosystem, if all values exchanged are captured, the system is optimally efficient. However, in many networks of businesses, a large number of values go un-captured, creating inefficiencies by lowering the incentive for the participant (that is meant to receive the value) to continue participating in the interaction. Thus, since one gets no kudos

[24] **DIRECTV.** DIRECTV: Refer a Friend. *DIRECTV.* [Online] May 31, 2011. [Cited: May 31, 2011.] http://www.directv.com/DTVAPP/referral/referralProgram.jsp.

from recommending a good movie or a good restaurant, one might be less inclined to continue providing recommendations.

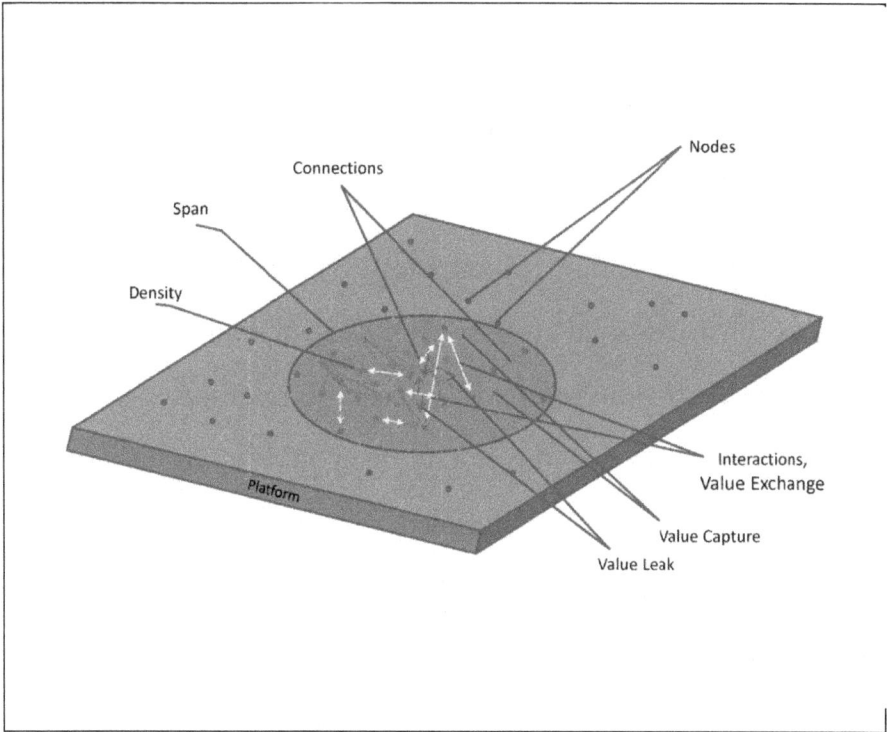

Figure 4 - Value Capture and Value Leak

Many businesses are built on a model of capturing difficult to capture values. Groupon captures the value of aggregating a critical mass of buyers to make a discounted transaction worthwhile to a business. Auto dealerships place loss-leader ads to capture prospective buyers' foot traffic. For a discussion that addresses the similarity of these strategies, see Surowiecki.[25]

Value Aggregation

The Groupon model illustrates another characteristic of a network with high potential value - value aggregation. If an individual approaches a restaurant and proposes that the restaurant provides him 100 certificates worth $20 of food and drinks each for a total sum of $800, but he will only pay the restaurant $800 if he is able to sell all 100 certificates by the next day for $10 each, the restaurant would be very skeptical that this promise will be fulfilled the next day. Groupon, however, has access to over 40 million subscribers as of this book's writing. Thus, its chances of finding enough buyers are dramatically higher, even if the number is divided into a much smaller group for a particular locale. The massive, almost instantaneous, and extremely low-cost aggregation of willing buyers for its deals allows Groupon to capture the value of buyer willingness and turn it into a significant value proposition that can compel transactions with the merchants.

---

[25] **Surowiecki, James.** Groupon Clipping. *The New Yorker.* December 20, 2010.

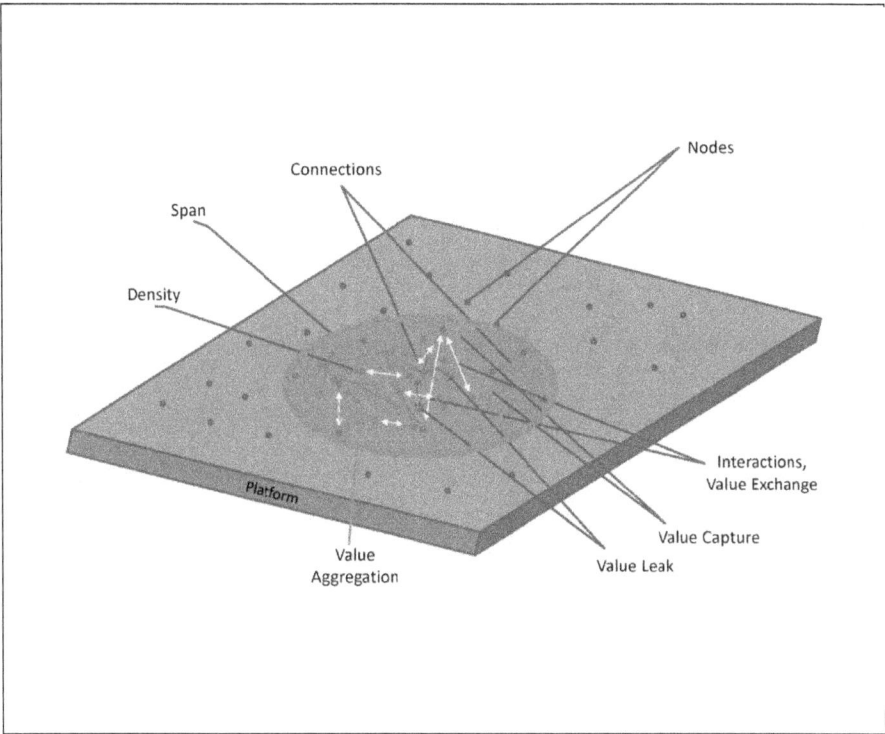

Figure 5 - Value Aggregation

Value Transformation

The Groupon example also illustrates value transformation. Without transforming buyers' willingness into guaranteed sales for merchants, Groupon would not be able to fulfill its end of the contract. Note, however, that there is a threshold - a critical mass - of sales that must be met before the deal can be consummated. Groupon cannot just assemble 10 willing buyers when the merchant needs 100 buyers to justify the discount he offers. The ability of a platform to aggregate values can be very important to its ability to transform values. Even in a traditional manufacturing environment, a critical number of the same components (e.g., nuts and bolts) must be aggregated for assembly into a finished product (e.g., automobile). In the digital world, aggregation can be performed dynamically, almost instantaneously, and with very little effort.

Value Alignment

Value alignment is a relatively complex, yet exciting topic, as it holds significant promise in helping re-invent a business's ecosystem. In many business networks, value exchange activities lack alignment and degrade the overall potential value of the networks. When two business partners mistrust each other and hedge their bets by not fully sharing technologies, the end products created together suffer. Misunderstandings are common in newly formed partnerships. If a buyer asks for a discount but is not willing to promise additional purchases later on, the supplier is less likely to acquiesce. A supplier may offer discounts if payment is made on time or ahead of time, but the buyer misses the due date. The discount may not be offered again, and the lack of discount, in turn, discourages the buyer from continuing business with the supplier.

Measures and detection techniques can be utilized to determine misalignments. Structures within the capital ecosystem can also be erected to encourage alignment. Within groups, norms and mores can communicate rules of engagement and set boundaries, helping to deter and contain misalignment and misunderstanding, as well as to foster trust, collaboration, and the development of public goods.

Formalizing Values

The next chapter formalizes values that are exchanged within a capital ecosystem by introducing a comprehensive capital taxonomy. A comprehensive capital taxonomy allows us to see how values are exchanged, created, captured, aggregated, and converted in a capital ecosystem. Sustainability of the ecosystem can thus be evaluated and anticipated from such a framework.

> "Don't look where you fall, but where you slipped."
>
> -African Proverb

3. The Capital Taxonomy

We previously introduced the concept of a capital ecosystem and the measurements that reflect its value potential. We define specifically a capital ecosystem as a network of interconnected participants who transact objects of values among each other. These objects of values may be tangible products, intangible products, or services. The receiver of an object of value reciprocates to the supplier an amount of capital, comprised of one or more types, that is deemed, within that particular transaction, to be of equal and fair value to the object received. In the context of this definition, value and capital are two sides of the same coin. That is, to gain value, one must give up capital or capitals. Such capitals are a proxy for the total amount of value one may obtain in a transaction, and value is a proxy for the capital or capitals one must surrender.

In a transaction, a buyer may, for example, argue that he or she "got a good deal" by paying in financial capital much less than what he or she received in value. However, our assumption is that from the other side of the transaction, the seller views the price to be fair. Otherwise, the seller would not consummate the transaction. Value is gained on both sides of the transaction as both buyer and seller feel that the total amounts of capitals they give up, from their corresponding perspectives, are less "valuable" than the values they obtained.

When we expand our concept of capital to more than just financial capital, a sense of completeness is achieved for transactions, as both perceived "cheap deals" and "expensive deals" are fair transactions.

Thus, we now present a comprehensive description of capital with different types of capitals to set the stage for a more in-depth exploration of value creation and, eventually, the sustainability of the value creation processes within a capital ecosystem.

Often a business owner instinctively believes in the worth or the value of her business and its prospects, but she cannot prove or disprove her belief. Surely, she thinks, there is more to the company than just what is in the financial statements. But how does she rigorously defend and justify this thought process?

The answer lies in the fact that capital must be viewed in many forms. Financial capital is but one type of capital. There are other types of capital such as intellectual capital and social capital, the former having been widely recognized for many years and the latter having recently come into more and more discussions as social networks have become pervasive.

There have been multiple efforts at creating a comprehensive capital taxonomy. One framework is the Five Capitals model, authored by the Forum for the Future.[26] The Five Capitals model presents that there are five types of capitals: natural capital, human capital, social capital, financial capital, and manufactured capital. Another framework is the Skandia Value Scheme, developed more than a decade ago by Lief

---

[26] **Forum for the Future.** The Five Capitals model. *Forum for the Future.* [Online] 2010. http://www.forumforthefuture.org/projects/the-five-capitals.

Edvinsson at Skandia AFS.[27]   The Skandia Value Scheme breaks overall capital into financial and intellectual capital. Intellectual capital is further divided into human capital and structural capital, which is composed of customer capital and organization capital.   The figure below shows the value scheme as a hierarchy.

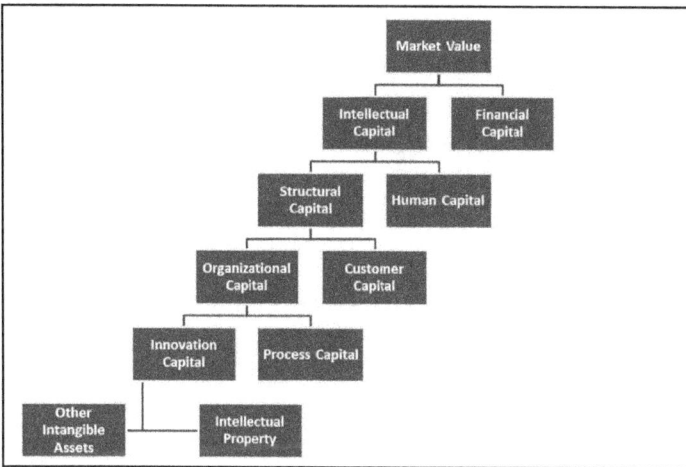

Figure 6 - The Skandia Value Scheme. Adapted from Edvinsson (1997).

Most capital classification schemes began as efforts to better understand and systematize intellectual capital.   These efforts have resulted in a number of developed standards by world-wide bodies to address the measurement of intellectual capital, and, in the process, evolve into an overarching framework that includes financial capital.

---

[27] **Edvinsson, Leif.** Developing intellectual capital at Skandia. 3, 1997, *Long Range Planning,* Vol. 30, pp. 363-373.

The World Intellectual Capital Initiative (WICI) was formed in 2007 to create "a global framework for measuring and reporting on intellectual assets and capital".[28] The Intellectual Capital Statement (InCaS) is a European effort "to understand the value and value the understanding of our 'know-how'".[29] Additionally, the American Institute of CPAs (AICPA) has begun participating with the WICI through its EBRC (Enhanced Business Reporting Consortium) group.[30]

Verna Allee, CEO of Value Networks, helps promote the concept of looking at a business's network in terms of values that are beyond financial.[31] Her work has helped numerous organizations and groups understand the role of knowledge and intangibles in the creation of financial values. Allee's publications have resulted in a movement to identify, understand, and assess the value of business networks.

Similarly, Professor Jaap Gordijn of Vrije Universiteit Amsterdam has been working on the e^{3}value methodology

---

[28] **WICI.** WICI. *WICI.* [Online] 2007. http://www.wici-global.com/.

[29] **InCaS.** InCaS. *InCaS.* [Online] 2010. http://www.incas-europe.org/index-en.htm.

[30] **AICPA.** EBRC. *AICPA.* [Online] 2005.
http://www.aicpa.org/InterestAreas/AccountingAndAuditing/Resources/EBR/Pages/EnhancedBusiness
ReportingConsortium.aspx.

[31] *Value Network Analysis and Value Conversion of Tangible and Intangible Assets.* **Allee.** s.l. : Emerald Insights, 2008. Journal of Intellectual Capital. pp. 5-24.

that helps model the roles of values in business design and innovation.[32] Work on business modeling and business model generation through ontology has also been pursued and practiced by Alexander Osterwalder and Yves Pigneur.[33] Many of these efforts have resulted in much deeper understanding of the drivers behind business value, and thus how business values of all kinds, financial and otherwise, are achieved. These values ultimately result in the growth of capitals that a company possesses, of which financial capital is a part.

For our discussion, we introduce a capital taxonomy that builds from the Skandia Value Scheme and seeks to comprehensively address the many forms of capitals to help formalize our subsequent exploration of capital creation in a capital ecosystem. *Figure 7* below provides an abridged visual of our capital taxonomy.

---

[32] **Gordijn, Jaap.** e3value. *e3value.* [Online] 2011. http://www.e3value.com/index.php.

[33] *An e-Business Model Ontology for Modeling e-Business.* **Osterwalder, Alexander and Pigneur, Yves.** Bled, Slovenia : s.n., 2002. 15th Bled Electronic Commerce Conference.

```
The Capital Taxonomy (abridged)

Natural Capital
Human Capital
Manufactured Capital
|_____ Tangible Capital
            |_____ Building Capital
            |_____ Machine Capital
            |_____ Human Consumable Capital
    |_____ Intangile Capital
            |_____ Financial Capital
                Intellectual Capital
                    |_____ Information Capital
                    |_____ Technology Capital
                Social Capital
```

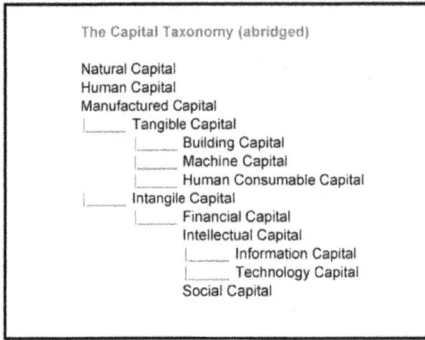

Figure 7 – An Abridged Capital Taxonomy

We further describe the types of capitals listed. The initiated reader can also extrapolate the breakdown of additional capital types, e.g., innovation capital being a subset of technology capital, and customer or relational capital being a subset of social capital. The capital taxonomy does not need to be exhaustive to facilitate the discussion of the value creation and desired sustainability of a capital ecosystem once there is an awareness of the different types of capitals that flow throughout such a network.

It is worth repeating that there are many types of capitals beyond financial. Oftentimes the non-financial capitals are the leading indicators of a company's prospects, as well as its overall health. Non-financial capitals also provide key competitive advantages to the firm, via management, culture and diversity. Just as importantly, non-financial capitals often provide the greatest barriers to entry to protect the firm's competitive position, as when intellectual capital is achieved in the form of a patent, or even a prototype of a new state-of-the-art product. Non-financial capitals are behind the breathtaking growth of some firms. Witness Apple and Salesforce.com.

Natural Capital

Natural capital is that which is naturally occurring, without any action on the part of the participant. Beyond the obvious tangible natural capitals such as land, minerals, iron deposits, oil, natural gas; citizenship, business climate, and culture are also examples of natural capital. Societal structures and organizational frameworks such as schools, youth groups (e.g., Girls Scouts, Big Brother, etc.) are natural capitals within a community that provide support and resiliency to a neighborhood.

Human Capital

Human capital refers to the exercise of human intellect or physicality to achieve some type of results. Manual labor is human capital, as is strategizing about how to acquire market share.

Manufactured Capital

Manufactured capital includes all types of capital that has been produced artificially. This includes tangibles such as buildings and machines, as well as intangibles such as money, information, relationships, and technology.

Tangible Capital

Tangible capital includes anything that is tangibly manufactured, ranging from automobiles and factories to frozen foods to laptops.

Intangible Capital

Intangible capital is anything artificially produced but only exists in virtual form and can only be witnessed via a representation. Examples include spreadsheets, dollar bills, business cards, and patents.

Information Capital

Information capital deserves a special discussion, as it pervades almost every aspect of our life and serves as proxy for an enormous number of different capitals, from website click-throughs to option contracts to a wireless patent. Information capital thus includes intellectual capital.

Information capital has many interesting characteristics. Information itself, when treated as an economic good, is governed by the theory of information economics.

As pointed out by Carl Shapiro and Hal Varian at UC Berkeley in their landmark book, *Information Rules: A Strategic Guide to the Network Economy*,[34] information is non-rivalrous and non-excludible, making it a public good. With zero marginal cost, information can be leveraged to multiply scale the values resulting from its utilization.

We will see that information capital is a significant, if not critical, part of almost every value exchange within a capital ecosystem. Beyond the obvious capital it provides, information serves as a proxy for many intangible values, ranging from stock ownership to click-throughs, and as signals that are critical in many market functions. The study of information as market signals earned George Akerlof, Michael

---

[34] **Shapiro, Carl and Varian, Hal.** *Information Rules: A Strategic Guide to the Network Economy.* Boston : HBS Press, 1999.

Spence, and Joseph E. Stiglitz the 2001 Nobel Prize in Economics.[35]

Negative Capitals

Just as different types of capitals can be accumulated, negative capitals can also exist by negating the values that have been acquired. Within a society where there is a high level of violence and within a country where there exists a high level of corruption, negative natural capital exists to sap away cultural and structural capitals accumulated. Similarly, negative information capital can exist in the form of distracting or conflicting data. When a company announces plans for products which it has no intention of pursuing, only to slow down the migration of customers to its rival, negative information signals are broadcasted and contribute to negative information capital that customers and prospects, as well as competitors, are receiving. A very common form of negative information capital exists in the case of a customer having to deal with multiple vendors that contribute to a product. When something breaks, the customer is told by one company that the problem is caused by the component from the other

---

[35] **Nobelprize.org.** The Prize in Economics 2001 - Press Release. *Nobelprize.org.* [Online] October 10, 2001. [Cited: May 31, 2011.]

company, and vice versa. The customer is left to bounce back and forth between the two companies without any clear resolution.

A Comprehensive Capital Balance Sheet

A comprehensive view of capitals points out a related concept, the concept of conversion rates among the capitals. One can see these capital conversions taking place during various economic cycles. In a recession, financial capital is scarce, and the exchange rate to financial capital is low. This explains why in bad economic times, large segments of population head back to school. These groups are focused on building their intellectual capital, so that, once economic growth and hiring pick up, the intellectual capital can be exchanged for financial capital at a higher rate, i.e., higher compensation.

For a business, a comprehensive capital balance sheet would indicate not only the financial capital balance but also the reserves of all other capitals. A comprehensive capital balance sheet can provide the full picture of the company's performance and provide useful leading indicators of financial performance.

Thus, similar to the efforts of the WICI and InCaS, it would be valuable for every firm to draft a comprehensive capital balance sheet, where not just financial capital is recorded, but all the other capitals in the taxonomy are estimated and validated as well, thereby taking stock of the true worth of the firm. In 2010, Harvard Business School (HBS) held a workshop on integrated reporting, attended by over 100 of the world's leading authorities on corporate disclosure and chaired by Professor Robert G. Eccles and with opening remarks from HBS dean Nitin Nohria. Integrated reporting addresses the concept of reporting on multiple capitals, as exemplified by White's paper, "The Five Capitals of Integrated Reporting: Toward a Holistic Architecture for Corporate Disclosure".[36] White listed the five capitals as intellectual capital, natural capital, financial capital, organizational capital, and social capital.

In the next chapter, the concept of capital transformation is introduced to demonstrate the power of non-financial capitals and set the stage for the illustration of wealth creation in the digital domain by innovative business models.

---

[36] *The Five Capitals of Integrated Reporting: Toward a Holistic Architecture for Corporate Disclosure.* **White, Allen L.** Boston : Harvard Business School, 2010.

4

"The expectations of life depend upon diligence; the mechanic that would perfect his work must first sharpen his tools."

-Confucius

4. Capital Transformation and Sustainability

E very business begins with a hypothesis of value gain. This is why almost every business model analysis begins with the question, "What is your value proposition?" Whether the value to be gained is financial profit, or the enjoyment of creating a first-class product, the proof of value gained does not exist until the first sale is made and then - if and only if - the total costs that went into making the product is less than the revenue realized from the sale. This thought exercise, however, may not be very helpful in explaining the many businesses (especially pure Internet plays) that charge much less than the total costs they incur to deliver their products or services. It is possible that the proprietor enjoys the process of product creation or service delivery and feels as though she validates the value of her business whether or not a customer pays an appropriate price. In this case, we posit that the capital the proprietor receives in exchange for delivering the product or service is not merely financial, but also includes social, intellectual, and other types of capital.

On the one hand, the hypothesis of value gain for a business must be tested before it can be considered viable or sustainable. On the other hand, all values involved must be considered, including non-financial values. Thus, the sustainability of a capital ecosystem must be validated with the value exchanges that occur within the ecosystem.

Capital Transformation

We previously stated that value and capital are two sides of the same coin, where value is what a party gains in a transaction, and capital is what it gives up to acquire the value. The capital that a firm possesses can exist in many forms, ranging from financial capital to social capital to intellectual capital. These capitals can be spent by the firm to acquire what it needs, from tangible things of value, such as machines and buildings, to intangibles such as information and reputation.

As the firm conducts its operations, producing its goods and/or services, capital is transformed from one form to another. Financial capital is spent to acquire labor capital, which in turn is spent to acquire tangible finished good capital or service capital to be delivered to customers, as measured, for example, by the number of hours a consulting firm delivers to its clients.

Capital transformation holds the key to the understanding of sustainability in a capital ecosystem. A business model is a representation of a capital ecosystem. By tracing the capitals that flow throughout the ecosystem and how they are transformed, one can test the viability of the capital ecosystem.

The simplest ecosystem involves a producer of goods and a buyer of those goods. The producer provides finished goods capital to the buyer and receives financial capital in return. Some ecosystems require more than two types of participants to achieve sustainability. The classical n-sided market is an example that comes to mind. Take for instance the Google capital ecosystem for search. An Internet user employs the search engine without any payment, i.e., without surrendering any financial capital. If the ecosystem involves only the user and Google, it would not be sustainable, as Google cannot provide the free service indefinitely. With the involvement of a third type of participant, the merchant who pays for the Google AdWords, the capital that the user gives up is her attention (or screen real estate) to the display of the merchant's description and website address. The merchant, in turn, gives up financial capital to Google, which, completing the loop, gives up search engine service capital to the user.

Within many typical capital ecosystems, the number of capital exchanges and the types of capitals being exchanged are numerous and can occur simultaneously at multiple levels among several types of participants. The figure below illustrates the exchanges of different capitals among the participants.

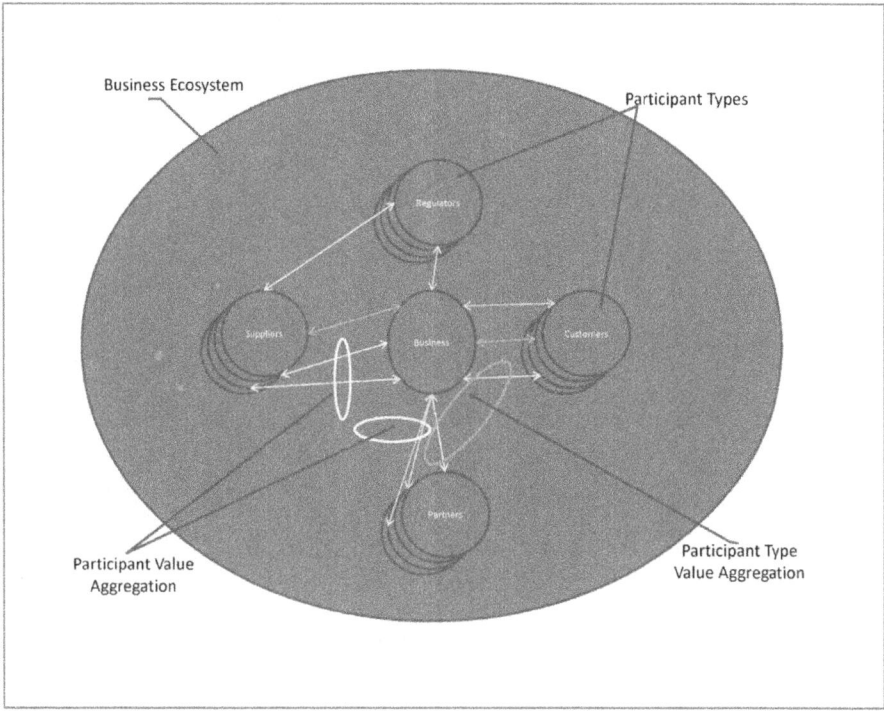

Figure 8 - Capital Exchanges Among Participants

Capital transformation accounts for the movements of different types of capitals across various types of participants. When a capital is transformed from one form to another form or a combination of other forms, a transformation factor exists, based on historical measures or on anticipated or guesstimated numbers.

As we earlier stated, some capital transformation requires a minimum amount of one form of capital before it can be transformed to another. For online traffic to be transformed to advertising dollars, there must be enough traffic in terms of CPM. We refer to this as the capital transformation threshold.

Sustainability

When participants are juxtaposed with the capital exchanges in which they participate, scenarios of sustainability can be explored and examined. Various sequences of consecutive state transitions can also be constructed to anticipate the ecosystem's eventual state.

For a capital ecosystem to be sustainable, the total capitals, in all forms, that each participant receives must be greater than the total capitals, in all forms, that it gives up. We can deduce from this that the net total capitals, in all forms, of a sustainable capital ecosystem must be positive.

If a participant in a particular capital ecosystem tracks all the forms of capitals that she exchanges with other participants in the ecosystem, and, based on the capital transformation rates, has a net positive total capital, that participant would be willing to continue being a part of the ecosystem. In simple and intuitive terms, we would say that the participant feels that she is getting good returns for her participation.

The goal of every capital ecosystem is to maximize the total net capital gain by all participants. The goal of each participant within the ecosystem is to maximize its net capital gain. To evaluate a firm's business model, one would analyze its capital ecosystem to determine first whether it maximizes its total net capital gain and secondly, whether the ecosystem is sustainable. Google's capital ecosystem includes many participants, ranging from users to merchants (who purchase AdWords), hardware suppliers, advertisers, and independent developers. While its capital ecosystem is sustainable because of net total capital gain, Google itself also experiences net capital gains.

Capital Exchange and Barrier to Entry

The amounts of different forms of capitals that a firm exchanges with other participants in its capital ecosystem serve as barriers to entry for new entrants, since the new entrants must be able to provide the same amounts of equivalent forms of capitals to the other participants. For example, the search value Google provides to an Internet user represents the required value a new entrant must provide to the user. Collectively the capitals that the firm exchanges with all other participants in its capital ecosystem serve as the total barrier to entry. The firm's capital ecosystem, if sustainable and optimal, help create a higher barrier to entry.

Overcoming Barriers to Entry

In the same way that sustainable capitals provided to participants in an ecosystem create barriers to entry, innovation of values provided to participants can break down the barriers. Disruptive technologies and disruptive business models do this by transforming, reinventing, and/or repackaging the capitals provided to the participants in their ecosystems, whether those participants are also parts of other capital ecosystems. To do this, disruptors must have new ways to:

- recognize heretofore unrecognized forms of capitals or new forms of capital and capital exchanges,

- capture the capitals,

- accumulate the capitals,

- transform the capitals

Attention capital has been known but was not formally captured and transformed until the Internet and companies such as Google, Yahoo and AOL came along. For many years, Nielsen television ratings provided approximate measures of audience size and attention. DoubleClick, one of the pioneers of Internet advertising which has since been acquired by Google, recognized and provided the value of advertising that is coordinated across vast web properties. DoubleClick also enables the accumulation of attention capital across websites to transform it into meaningful advertising revenue for the owners of multiple websites. Eyeball capital has always been known, as we can see from freeway advertisements, but what DoubleClick and Internet advertising have done is to provide a way to accumulate and transform the caught glances to financial capital without requiring the investment in roadway signs. It does this more efficiently and accountably by orders of magnitude more efficiently and accountably.

It is worth reiterating that capital transformation is the conversion of capital from one form to another in support of the sustainability of the capital ecosystem. In subsequent chapters, we outline a framework around this concept to create viable business models that are based on sustainable capital ecosystems. We further provide strategies to optimize the capital ecosystem as well as the business model.

Key Capital Exchanges

We discuss below some typical capital exchanges based on interactions with common types of participants and how these exchanges can help sustain the ecosystem.

With Customers

With customers, a business entity exchanges finished goods or services for financial capital. Beyond this basic exchange, the business may also exchange information capital with its customers. It provides customers with information on products, warranties, support, etc., and, in return, receives information from customers related to their usage of the product, satisfaction, intentions of repeat purchases, design feedback, as well as referrals. The product warranty also provides the customer peace of mind and signals the commitment and credibility of the manufacturer.

With the advent of customer relationship management (CRM) software, multiple touch-points with customers are recognized and tapped. A community of customers can help to enhance the product use experience, create an environment for additional values, needs, and demands; and harness the power of customer referrals and testimonials. These non-financial capital exchanges can help sustain a capital ecosystem that, with financial capital exchange alone, cannot survive. Zappos.com is a clear example. How does Zappos.com afford the 2-way free shipping and unconditional returns? It has learned to harness customer satisfaction, word-of-mouth advertisement, and loyalty to make up for those cost-of-sales expenses.[37]

With Suppliers

As the converse of the customer relationship, a business provides financial capital to its suppliers and receives materials or services in return. But just as with customers, there are many more capital exchanges that take place. Again, information constitutes a key capital exchanged between a business and its suppliers. The advent of information systems have allowed companies to communicate directly, and in many cases, automatically, to their suppliers when certain stock materials are low. Some companies go further and provide production forecasts to their suppliers to facilitate efficient just-in-time processing, keeping low inventories of materials that may spoil or decay. Even further, many retailers employ drop-ship logistics and hold no inventory. This strategy can

---

[37] **Hsieh, Tony.** *Delivering Happiness: A Path to Profits, Passion, and Purpose.* New York : Business Plus, 2010.

only be achieved with information sharing and coordination with suppliers.

Suppliers in return can provide additional services that go beyond financial capital or the typical finished goods and primary services that were initially part of the contract. For example, suppliers may place goods on consignment and provide catalog services to a business's customers. Suppliers may also provide branding services via product especially tailored for the business's brand to help the business achieve differentiation.

Retailers both online and offline (Amazon, Best Buy, etc.) have utilized branded products from their suppliers in order to differentiate their products not only for branding value but also to prevent price comparison. Best Buy, for example, sells devices from Dell branded exclusively for Best Buy. Amazon sells many televisions at sale prices which it is not allowed to display. In this case, Amazon receives information from the supplier, i.e., minimum advertised price. Xignite, an online provider of data as a service, supplies data distribution services to various companies that are branded to appear and behave as though they were provided by the companies themselves.[38] Another example is virtual office space. There are virtual offices for rent at low monthly rates, providing prestigious addresses and receptionist services, while entailing no physical space, to provide businesses that don't need physical office space with a differentiating location.[39]

With Partners

Information is a key value exchange between partners in an ecosystem. Some partnerships even exchange technologies, as well as staff. Most partnerships involve multiple exchanges of multiple forms of capital. Relational capital is also often exchanged between partners when they refer each other to customers and bring each other into deals.

The understanding of the different forms of capitals being exchanged is important in order to establish partnership boundaries and to minimize conflicts of interests. Oracle, for example, licenses the ARIS toolset from IDS Scheer for its Oracle BPA suite. SAP, a direct competitor of Oracle, also

---

[38] **Xignite.** NASDAQ and Xignite to Provide On-Demand Tick Data via Cloud Computing Platform: Xignite Press. *Xignite.* [Online] June 22, 2010. [Cited: May 31, 2011.] http://www.xignite.com/News/PressRelease.aspx?articleid=215.

[39] **Wikipedia.** Virtual Office - Wikipedia. *Wikipedia.* [Online] May 31, 2011. [Cited: May 31, 2011.] http://en.wikipedia.org/wiki/Virtual_office.

licenses ARIS for its SAP Enterprise Modeling. The information and intellectual capital exchanged between IDS Scheer and both of its partners, who are direct competitors, must have constraints to keep the relationships sustainable.[40] The constraints are implementable only with an understanding of the different types of capitals the partners do exchange and do not exchange.

With Regulating Bodies

Regulating bodies are seen typically as agencies that require information capital from businesses to monitor them for compliance. What is seldom taken into account is the branding and differentiation value that these agencies' stamps of compliance and recognition provide to the business. The International Standards Organization (ISO), for example, uses its ISO standards to provide signals of high standards about companies' manufacturing practices, thus providing branding and differentiation capitals.[41] The GSA Schedule program is another example of regulating bodies providing differentiation

---

[40] **Roediger, Uwe.** How Oracle BPA Suite and generic ARIS Platform products play together. *ARIS Community.* [Online] August 17, 2009. [Cited: May 31, 2011.]
http://www.ariscommunity.com/print/users/uro/2009-08-17-how-oracle-bpa-suite-and-generic-aris-platform-products-play-together.

[41] **The British Assessment Bureau.** ISO 9001 proven to help win new business . *The British Assessment Bureau.* [Online] May 25, 2011. [Cited: May 31, 2011.] http://www.british-assessment.co.uk/news-story.asp?newsTitle=ISO-9001-proven-to-help-win-new-business-.

capital through a seal of approval in exchange for compliance to their published standards and vetting procedures.[42]

[42] **Brown, Steven.** How GSA Schedule takes your Brand Name Ahead . *Amazines.* [Online] June 8, 2011. [Cited: June 10, 2011.] http://www.amazines.com/article_detail.cfm?articleid=2944565.

5

> "Few things are harder to put up with than the annoyance of a good example."
>
> -Mark Twain

5. Living Proofs

I n this chapter we explore the capital ecosystems of some well-known digital businesses, as well as a traditional business that brilliantly demonstrates the concept of capital transformation - 7-Eleven. We discuss their business models in the context of their ecosystems and our capital transformation framework, exploring their capital exchanges with other ecosystem participants, their capital accumulation platform, and their capital transformation strategies. These businesses are living proof of sustained high-value and well-aligned capital ecosystems.

Hotmail

We begin our discussion with Hotmail because it provides a clean example of capital ecosystem expansion for sustainability. It also concisely illustrates the concepts of capital accumulation and capital transformation.

Hotmail is now part of Microsoft after Sabeer Bhatia and Jack Smith sold the firm to Microsoft for $400 million in 1997, less than 2 years after they started the company.[43]

Hotmail's ecosystem consisted of 3 main participant types: the email service provider (i.e., Hotmail), the user, and the advertisers. If the ecosystem had consisted of only the email service provider and the user, Hotmail would just be another supplier providing email service and a mail reader to its users (though web-based email was a novelty at the time) to its users, receiving in return financial capital. Hotmail created another participant type out of the users, mainly the users' network of contacts. Hotmail also added advertisers as the 4th participant type. The idea of including advertisers in the ecosystem was, however, not new at the time. The unique feature of Hotmail's business model then was the embedding

---

[43] **Penenberg, Adam.** *Viral Loop.* New York : Hyperion, 2009.

of the message "Get your free email at Hotmail" at the bottom of every email.

What they did not only made the idea of Hotmail viral, but also enlarge their ecosystem to every outer limit that their email traveled. Each Hotmail email that is sent, received, and read is an advertisement for Hotmail, effectively creating an ad system spanning millions of nodes globally and possibly everywhere that the Internet exists. Whenever Hotmail is used, advertisements appear, effectively collecting eyeballs for advertisers.

One user reading a Hotmail glancing at the advertising does not mean much, but millions of users with tens of millions of glances allowed Hotmail to collect the attention capital and transform it to financial capital via advertising dollars. The embedment of a brand signal or links back to the provider of the message exchange is now a widely used technique, as we everyday see in email messages with the end-phrase "Sent from my iPhone."

Google

Google's business model has been studied, dissected, imitated, applied, vilified and envied because of its astounding success.

Google's primary capital ecosystem includes the search engine provider, the search users, and advertisers. Google provides search service value to the users and receives in return, attention capital, which, when aggregated, becomes traffic. Google then takes this traffic capital and converts it to financial capital through advertisers. Advertisers gives up financial capital to gain traffic capital from Google, then translate the traffic into sales, achieving their own financial capital.

Facebook

Facebook's ecosystem is more complex yet extremely powerful, a recognition highlighted by the company's stratospheric valuation.

The power of Facebook's ecosystem lies in the almost complete containment of its ecosystem within the company's platform. The Facebook platform contains the interactions and almost every click of its estimated 800 million members. A user leaves the Google search engine every time he or she clicks on the link of a search result or an advertiser's website, whereas Facebook users almost never leave Facebook, except when they click on a link that sends them to a website completely unconnected to Facebook. A Facebook user has a choice to leave the Facebook platform just as a Google user does, yet because Facebook as a platform provides almost everything the member needs to message, interact, congregate online, and play games; almost every action and interaction is observable by Facebook.

This contained environment allows Facebook to gain a tremendous amount of information about its members, making it possible for them to execute pinpoint marketing and providing complete control over the majority of its ecosystem.

Moreover, unwilling to cede a piece of its ecosystem to the outside world, Facebook even began to extend its reach beyond its own platform. The introduction of Facebook Like allows members to not only register to Facebook websites they enjoy but also to reach back to the Facebook platform from wherever they frequent, effectively planting a Facebook flag at those sites. These sites are then part of the Facebook digital grid.

Because of the many participant types involved, the Facebook ecosystem is complex. There are members, advertisers, companies, service providers, and developers (such as game producers) and, of course, Facebook itself. Facebook continues to feed the participants of its ecosystem the capitals they need, allowing them to create and exchange even more capitals and; eventually benefiting Facebook again. To the advertisers, Facebook provides analytics for business intelligence capital for targeted marketing. To the developers, it provides relational capitals in the form of a 800-million-plus-people user base, as well as information about these users for suitable applications. To companies, it provides virtual real estate, for flag-planting locations, encouraging users to "friend" their products and companies. Because it has an incredible amount of information about its members, Facebook is by far the most targeted advertising environment available. With more than 800 million members, network effects make Facebook a requirement to connect with friends online. Facebook's continually innovative interaction platform reinforces the value of virtual connection.

Facebook provides a variety of values to its members, ranging from social connection to entertainment, search, organization, and broadcasting. In return for all these values, Facebook receives the members' interaction capital. Not just attention capital, but interaction capital. Members' conversations, photos, videos, group discussions, and random musings are observed and recorded by Facebook. The interaction capital can be transformed to a myriad of other capitals, from targeted advertising information to preferences for games that can be fed to developers of services on the Facebook platform. Though interactions on Facebook are virtual, they can achieve such parity of importance with their offline counterpart that Facebook can sell a virtual flower for real money. Even more profitable for Facebook is, however, Facebook Credits, where the virtual currency can be transformed even more easily to values within the ecosystem (such as game-playing time) and to real money. Recall our discussion of transitions. Facebook Credits provide a smoother transition from virtual interactions to financial capital.

Most of the capitals that Facebook aggregates cannot be realized without the 5 key characteristics that are important to the value of a capital ecosystem. Facebook has very high density, of course, with more than 800 million members. The density is increased beyond the 800 million members because there are groups and companies within Facebook that have members and fans. This provides another layer of density. Add to that the ability to search within Facebook, allowing members or organizations to target and communicate with any group or subgroup of entities.

There are high levels of interactions among members in Facebook, as evidenced not only by reports of people spending hours a day on Facebook, but also by the constant update stream of happenings within one's network of friends.

Capital exchange is high, though most of the capitals exchanged currently are not of financial nature. The exchange of entertainment capital, of social capital, and of information capital is extremely high throughout Facebook.

As a "closed" platform, Facebook is able to capture, accumulate, and repository most of the capitals via information, i.e., its record of interactions. It is able to track, retain and accumulate social capital, relational capital, information capital, and intellectual capital.

Facebook has demonstrated its ability to transform information capital to financial capital through payments from marketers. It has demonstrated the ability to transform social capital to financial capital through virtual gifts. It also demonstrated the ability to transform its own relational capital to social capital for game and service developers on its platform.

It is impossible to ignore the incredible value potential of the Facebook capital ecosystem. To the degree that investors feel they can substantiate the values within this ecosystem, they have assigned a staggering financial valuation to Facebook of $65 billion as of this writing.[44]

Xignite

Since its founding in 2000, Xignite has grown into the market leader in on-demand financial market data distribution—fulfilling more than 5 billion web service requests monthly.[45] Xignite was founded to address one of the key issues for business software applications, integration of various business systems from different vendors. True to our recognition earlier that business must be agile and responsive to results of experimentation, what started as an "interface marketplace" took advantage of the disruptive standards and technologies of XML, just emerging at the time, refocused itself on data integration and exchange. XML enables the programmatic integration of software and their data, allowing for the virtualization of data integration operations. Virtualization lets

---

[44] **Farber, David.** Latest Facebook Investment Values Company at $65 Billion - CNBC. *CNBC.* [Online] May 3, 2011. [Cited: May 31, 2011.]

[45] **Xignite.** NASDAQ'S "Big Data" Cloud Service Launches on Xignite's Platform. *Xignite.* [Online] April 26, 2011. [Cited: May 31, 2011.]

Xignite leverage on information capital's non-rivalrous nature, replicating one stream of data into several and enabling multiple users to connect to and make use of the data almost instantaneously. What took weeks or months before can now be done in minutes.

Because of information capital's non-rivalrous nature and economies of replication, Xignite's value proposition grows with the span and density of its network. Its ecosystem consists of Xignite, its data providers or partners, and its customers. The financial capital that Xignite receives from any one customer is too small of an amount to justify the building of a traditional data interface. However, with a large number of customers for a data stream, the combined financial capital stream is large enough to justify building an infrastructure and the capabilities to derive useful data streams from one original set of data. The key driver behind Xignite's success is, however, the use of new technology to increase the span and density of its ecosystem. On the demand side, Xignite increases span and density by enabling data users who were never before able to afford, both financially and technically, to buy data. On the supply side, the technology allows Xignite to put into use data streams that have long been locked up behind the data producers' and providers' walls since it took an enormous amount of effort to provision that data to potential users in the outside world. Another key trend that played into Xignite's ecosystem, is the low level of friction that the Internet offers in the transfer of data. What used to require weeks and months to provision as a private data interchange can now be done in seconds over the Internet.

The lower friction extends to even the traditional function of business of billing, receivables management, and collection. Xignite's customers can subscribe to its service and pay online automatically with each request of data, enabling Xignite to carry very little receivables and spend almost no effort in collection. The initiated reader can probably identify this effort as part of the value leaks in the value exchanges between traditional data providers and their customers.

Xignite's leverage of the non-rivalrous nature and low-replication cost of information capital is a strategy relied upon by numerous online, hybrid, and traditional businesses, ranging from infomediaries to platform providers. For example, Netflix utilizes the same model to distribute videos over the Internet, with monthly automatic payments from customers for their Netflix accounts.[46]   Apple iTunes

[46] **Asharya, Kat.** Netflix Moves Towards Streaming-Only Services. *ITVedia.* [Online] January 19, 2011. [Cited: May 31, 2011.] http://www.itvedia.com/news/1047.html.

distributes music all over the world via numerous devices by replicating and splicing songs from albums for millions of subscribers.[47] The costs of packaging information into consumable units are dramatically lower than that of the traditional cut-and-paste process of the printing press, so much so that the entire newspaper industry has been disrupted.[48]

7-Eleven

7-Eleven is a traditional business that beautifully illustrates the concept of value transformation and makes the case for value transformation that can be achieved with or without digital technologies.

7-Elven was founded in 1927 as the Southland Ice Company in Dallas, Texas. Its stores stay open on Sundays and in the evenings when other grocery stores at the time were closed. The name 7-Eleven was adopted to reflect the unheard-of (at the time) store hours from 7 AM in the morning to 11 PM in the evening. The company and its franchisees now operate over 33,000 stores globally. Its ubiquity and always-open

[47] **Wikipedia.** iTunes Store - Wikipedia. *Wikipedia.* [Online] June 11, 2011. [Cited: June 11, 2011.] http://en.wikipedia.org/wiki/ITunes_Store.

[48] **Anthony, Scott D and Gilbert , Clark G.** Can the Newspaper Industry Stare Disruption in the Face? *Nieman Reports.* Spring 2006.

policy provides a unique value of convenience to customers.[49] 7-Eleven's primary product is not coffee or the newspaper, but convenience. On the demand side, the company charges customers a calculated premium for items (versus grocery stores, for example). On the supply side, the company operates a dense and coordinated network of retail locations and logistics to transform operational activities into convenience capital. To operate such a vast network of retail stores on a 24-hour basis demands extreme scheduling and logistical capabilities. McDonald utilizes 7-Eleven's convenience strategy by using the 24-hour operating schedule to up the ante in the fast food industry. Though not the critical part, the franchise model also plays significantly into the creation of convenience capital. Without franchisees, 7-Eleven would not be able to achieve ubiquity as quickly to complete the convenience proposition.

The 7-Eleven ecosystem thus includes four primary participant types: the customers, the franchise, the franchisees, and the suppliers. This ecosystem is like any other franchise's ecosystem. However, because of its goal of convenience, 7-Eleven's logistics serves as the key catalyst for interactions and value exchanges. McDonald's, while allocating appropriate

---

[49] **7-Eleven, Inc.** History. *7-Eleven Corporate.* [Online] April 2011. http://corp.7-eleven.com.

importance to logistics, also relies on quality control and product mixes, as convenience is not its key value proposition. We are able to tolerate at times the quality of certain 7-Eleven stores' coffee and snacks, because we know that we can ways get headache medicine at the store at any hour. We are not as tolerant of bad fries, because we typically have hunger pangs at approximately the same time each day, when our neighborhood McDonald's stores are normally open.

"To see a World in a Grain of Sand
And a Heaven in a Wild Flower,
Hold Infinity in the palm of your hand
And Eternity in an hour."

-William Blake

6. Digital Strategies

Many successful digital strategies derive their power from common elements that we have discussed. Social bookmarking, for instance, utilizes the power of crowds to create value in bookmarks.[50] Crowdsourcing, in general, describes strategies that employ the power of crowds for the creation of various types of capitals, aggregate the capital units created, and convert them to other capitals.[51] Crowdfunding applies the power of crowds to financing, with the proposition that many supporters of a project, while contributing small amounts, when gathered and aggregated, will create a critical mass of

---

[50] **Tony, Hammond, et al., et al.** Social Bookmarking Tools (I): A General Overview. *D-Lib Magazine.* April 2005.

[51] **Howe, Jeff.** The Rise of Crowdsourcing . *Wired.* June 2006.

capital.[52] As a matter of fact, almost all strategies employ the various components of the capital ecosystem value engine. Groupon and Kickstarter, for instance, employ the creation of contracts that support a value state, then catalyze transitions to that state. Kickstarter goes even further and provides up-to-date metrics on the transitions, i.e., how much fund has thus far been raised for a project.[53] This transparency helps fuel transitions; that is, perhaps one is on the fence about funding the project, but sees that it has picked up quite a few investments. One thus reasons that perhaps there is more merit to this project than previously thought.

The strategies inevitably serve to catalyze transitions in a capital ecosystem toward more density, interactions, and value exchanges. They also leverage each of the capital ecosystem's value management activities: capture, aggregate, transform, and multiply the collective capitals. The creativity demonstrated by the strategies in developing and implementing the catalysts are not just born out of theoretical and logical reasoning, but are also rooted in an understanding of the participants' psychology and perception of values. The

[52] **Economist, the.** Putting your money where your mouse is. *The Economist.* September 2, 2010.

[53] **Warren, Christina.** A Guide to Kickstarter & Crowd Funding [INFOGRAPHIC]. *Mashable.* [Online] January 17, 2011. [Cited: May 31, 2011.] http://mashable.com/2011/01/17/kickstarter-crowd-funding-infographic/.

strategies also derive much of their power from the disruption enabled by technology and global interconnections, which are constantly developing at breakneck speed. Many of the business models owe their success to the agility of the virtual business environment. The digital components of these businesses are not only able to instantly respond to the market constraints, customer expectations, and economic factors, but also derive their power and efficiency from the "digitization" of the business.

We now discuss the evolution of well-known digital strategies against the backdrop of our framework of capital ecosystem and sustainability, examining the process by which the strategies help the network increase its value potential and the aggregation and transformation of capitals as a result. Many of these digital strategies, while critical to digital businesses, are usable and enormously beneficial to all types of businesses, including hybrid and traditional.

A Digital Strategy Timeline

The Internet was first the market ground for companies that offer "internetworking" and access tools. They were the networking equipment providers such as Cisco and Synoptics, the ISPs (Internet Service Providers) such as AOL and Earthlink, and the software providers such as Netscape (Navigator) and Microsoft (Internet Explorer). The subsequent period of growth saw companies such as Yahoo, CNET, and WebMD. Yahoo provided a directory, then a search engine, and served as an infomediary, directing Internet traffic to useful and interesting destinations. As the search engine war heated up, we saw the emergence of Lycos, Northern Light, and Alta Vista. Around this same time period, companies such as eBay, Amazon, and Buy.com became the new economy's darlings. These companies provide a platform for specific tasks, whether it is to buy, sell, or exchange goods. E-tailers were the rage during this time, fueling the dotcom bubble. Commerce was the next digital frontier, after digital plumbing and tools. Etailers invade almost every aspect of retailing from selling books (Amazon) to selling cars (Carsdirect) to trading stocks (Etrade). But communication, trade, and retailing relied on security to flourish, addressed by the emergence of companies such as RSA Security, Verisign, and the all-important PayPal, which created a secured way to transfer money over the Internet. The next digital frontier saw the emergence of the first communities. These included The Globe, WebMD, and iVillage. Their value propositions rely on community and advertising. However, their monetization models were not mature enough and member numbers were not high enough for adequate capital aggregation to offset the higher costs of operating an Internet company at the time. Their ability to raise venture capital (VC) money and achieve initial public offerings (IPO) was based on theoretical numbers. These companies were financially viable and profitable for the founders and seed investors while the dotcom bubble lasted. As operating costs decrease and access costs for users all over the world became less of a barrier, the second iteration of communities emerge with a clearer plan for monetization, lower costs of operations, higher membership, and actual monetization metrics to support their claims. At the same time, thanks to Google's AdWords, Internet advertising gained legitimacy. This became the era of Friendster, Myspace, MSN, Orkut, LinkedIn, and Facebook. These businesses amass unheard of numbers in members, on the order of tens of millions. As of this writing, the Facebook community includes over 800 million members. An interesting sub-strategy arises out of the success of the current crop of communities. Because of the large numbers of users they have gathered, they also serve as platforms. Amazon is no longer an e-tailer of books, but a platform for selling everything from books to batteries. Facebook became a platform for game developers, social media tools, and virtual gifts, as well as virtual currencies. Myspace became the launching pad for musicians and virtual celebrities. YouTube is currently the undisputed king in launching careers of unknown talents online. There was even the story of 17-year-old Ashley Qualls making more than $1 million a year and employing her mother and friends in her company making backgrounds for Myspace pages.[54] Without the critical and sustainable span, density, interactions, and value exchanges, communities would not be able to serve as platforms, since there would not be adequate value exchanges for the businesses deployed on them to aggregate and monetize values.

Even though each strategy seems to have its era, innovative companies continue to emerge via a particular strategy whether that strategy is the new fashion or an established approach. Mozilla Firefox and Safari web browsers still emerge even though Internet Explorer dominates the market. Google re-invented search even while Lycos, Yahoo (Inktomi), and Alta Vista were dominating. Twitter carved out

---

[54] **Salter, Chuck.** Girl Power. *Fast Company.* September 1, 2007.

its niche as a platform despite the dominance of Facebook, LinkedIn, Myspace, and Tencent. Others employ similar strategies in different industries or markets. Salesforce.com employs the platform strategy for software development. Netflix does the same for videos. What is interesting, however, is the unique make-up of these companies' ecosystems, which allows them to import the strategies learned elsewhere into their markets successfully. Additionally because of their unique ecosystems, they also blend in multiple strategies, making the mix of their business models extremely adaptable, responsive, and value-opportunistic. For example, Netflix not only employs the platform strategy, but also the analytics strategy. Netflix re-invented the video delivery business, but it applied the analytics strategy in capturing profits from segments of members with willingness to pay and exhibit certain price insensitivities. LinkedIn similarly leverages the analytics strategy in charging recruiters and premium users while providing free service to attract a massive user base.[55] The massive user base, in return, of course, makes recruiting and other LinkedIn premium services more compelling. Salesforce.com was supposed to be software over the Internet, allowing the customers to bypass installation,

---

[55] **Shuen, Amy.** *Web 2.0: A Strategy Guide.* Sebastopol : O'Reilly Media, 2008.

maintenance, and hardware infrastructure. Its infrastructure, however, allows other software to be developed and connect to it as a platform for customers and partners, helping the company leverage its entry into the cloud computing market. Amazon's famous web services platforms EC2 and S3 grew out of the company's developed capability and experience in massive online retailing.[56]

The timeline of Internet businesses have recently moved to the substantiated value proposition model, popularized by companies such as Groupon and Kickstarter. A great number of business models have also been based on plugging into the ecosystems of successful companies. GetGlue plugs into the ecosystems of Facebook and Twitter. Many mobile advertising agencies plug into the ecosystems of the iPhone, iPad, and Android devices. Video advertising firms plug into the ecosystem of YouTube and Vimeo. Of course, many software developers, hundreds of thousands of them, readily and willingly plug into the ecosystems of Apple's mobile devices and Google's Android through their apps marketplaces. Plug-ins and the combinations of multiple paradigms are an outgrowth of the mash-up concepts.

---

[56] **Wikipedia.** Amazon Web Services - Wikipedia. *Wikipedia.* [Online] May 4, 2011. [Cited: May 31, 2011.] http://en.wikipedia.org/wiki/Amazon_Web_Services.

Foursquare "mashes up" location-based services (LBS) with game, creating augmented reality, as when, for example, its members check into a location frequently enough to become "mayors."

The number of start-ups that are funded to support the ecosystems of companies great and small built on the primary strategies that we will discuss below is almost overwhelming. Of course, those that have gained traction get enormous valuations, as well as numerous copycats.

What is important to our task at hand is the recognition that capital ecosystems will only proliferate and widen, become at once more complex and more valuable. New tools and strategies are needed to invent, re-invent, monitor, and leverage capital ecosystems. That will be the focus of our last three chapters. Let us now discuss digital strategies according to the successive eras of the digital economy.

Internetworking Strategies

It can be said that the era of the Internet began in 1969, when ARPANET was born as the very first internetwork, created from the connection of 4 computer nodes, linking UCLA, Stanford Research Institute (SRI), UCSB, and the University of Utah.[57] Companies such as AT&T and IBM were built on the simple strategy of providing computing capabilities and technologies to connect the machines.

Access Strategies

Once internetworking became a reality, companies providing access to the Internet benefit from the demand for this new man-made wonder. Access allows early adopters to experiment, dream, and plan for a new future. Most values accessed by these adopters were non-financial, such as for scientific research, communication, etc. These values, however, were overwhelmingly justified by the speed, convenience, and novelty of the new environment, allowing access companies to reap enormous financial capitals in return, so much so that AOL could afford to send multiple CD's of ISP software directly to millions of household in the US.

The darlings of the early access era were the dial-up internet service providers (ISPs) like AOL, Earthlink, and Compuserve, as well as the telephone companies, as they hold the chokepoints of the new and disruptive platform. The sustainability of these companies' ecosystems depends on

[57] **Zakon, Robert H'obbes'.** Hobbes' Internet Timeline 10.1. *Hobbes' Internet Timeline.* [Online] December 15, 2010. [Cited: May 31, 2011.] http://www.zakon.org/robert/internet/timeline/.

massive numbers of users. Network effects began to take place, as more people accessed the larger and ever-more-real new environment, which, in turn, enticed more people to adopt. This positive feedback loop continued to drive demand for the Internet, demand for bigger "pipes," and better "on-ramps" to the new digital frontier.

Bandwidth and Plumbing Strategies

The bandwidth and plumbing companies are thus welcomed with open arms. With their advanced equipment, these companies can offer larger bandwidth, faster switches, higher reliability, and, to top it all off, lower costs per unit. Enter Intel, Cisco, Synoptics, Level 3 Communications, Global Crossing, AT&T, Cox, Covad, and other long-distance fiber providers. Not only do these companies address access demands, they also stimulate demand and increase supply by enabling a whole new set of websites to be created inexpensively and quickly (relatively speaking at the time). This strategy requires original engineering research and development. Great amounts of capitals were captured by these companies because multiple layers of connections and interactions were clamoring to be created, and they hold the key to capital exchanges and digital leverage. Many useful services were already conceived before bandwidth and user interfaces were even available to support them. The ecosystem of this strategy involves the simple exchange of technology capital for financial capital.

Because it relies heavily on research and development, only a handful of large and well capitalized companies (both financially and technologically) can afford to compete on this strategy, e.g., Cisco, Intel, Apple, Broadcom, and LinkSys. In terms of their ecosystems, these companies rely on the continued demand for digital bandwidth and connection. Wired bandwidth was supplemented, and at times replaced, by wireless bandwidth. Demand continued to be driven by new and novel applications such as video conferencing, video download, security, wireless technologies (e.g., Bluetooth), and wireless devices. It thus behooved plumbing providers to encourage additional bandwidth consumption by encouraging application development and the creation of interconnected networks, utilizing network effects.

User Access Tools Strategies

As adopters hopped on to the Internet in droves, if only for basic services such as Telnet and email, the potential for the new digital frontier continued to captivate. Imagination and visions of the new land ensued, and the need for ease-of-use and ease-of-access came to the forefront as visionaries foresaw the main wave of users that normally follow early adopters. Tools such as NCSA Mosaic browser, Netscape Navigator, and Internet Explorer hold the keys to capturing unheard of intellectual, relational, and interaction capital on the Internet. In a positive feedback loop, as more users were enticed by the new user interface, the demand to access the new landscape grew since everyone wanted to be where everyone else was. Additionally, the new tools only served to stoke more visions and imaginings for more applications, services, and capabilities such as exchanging pictures, downloading files, and accessing emails (as Hotmail later proved).

The ecosystems for tool companies, though seemingly simple, were convoluted, as traditional software companies anticipate the shift of use from personal and corporate confines to a global environment. Netscape thought the value proposition for its browser was a cinch, providing incredible amount of access and intellectual capital for a measly sum of $29 per browser, so it did not address competitive threats to its ecosystem from traditional software companies such as

Microsoft. Netscape did not anticipate the demands of one of the key participant types in its ecosystem: the personal computer makers. Microsoft, by taking the computer makers out of play from Netscape's ecosystem (by illegally forcing them to bundle Internet Explorer with the Windows operating system), cuts off the primary source of Netscape revenue.[58] The lesson demonstrated is that companies must continually monitor and scenario-play their ecosystem sustainability to ensure that each participant in the ecosystem cannot be enticed away by a higher net-capital gain within another ecosystem.

Infrastructure Strategies

Infrastructure companies such as AT&T, Sprint, Verizon, Cox, Level 3 Communications, and Global Crossing relied on the monetization of the infrastructure in which they have invested. A supportive ecosystem for them would include large numbers of applications and services requiring bandwidth. Thus encouraging bandwidth consumption through smart devices, online storage, and multimedia services would be in these companies' interest. They would also want

---

[58] *U.S v. Microsoft: Court's Findings of Fact*, 98-1232, s.l. : THE UNITED STATES DISTRICT COURT FOR THE DISTRICT OF COLUMBIA , November 5, 1999.

to include in their ecosystems firms that provide security in communication and interactions in order to build trust with users and thus reduce friction in value exchanges.

Infrastructure for the digital economy is as important as utilities such as water and electricity because almost every activity depends on it. Thus the competition for infrastructure continues to the present day, as still a major portion of the world's population needs access to the Internet, and new applications and layers of value exchanges continue to drive demands for bandwidth. In many ways the market seems saturated, but in a number of ways, there is still much more market to be developed.

Internet Services Strategies

The availability of access, plumbing, infrastructure, and user tools make it possible for just ideas to be implemented and played out in the new frontier of the Internet. At this point, anyone with a bright idea in a garage can single-handedly create a multi-million-dollar business, and many have. Many ideas began as nothing more than hobbies, since no great technological breakthroughs in hardware, real estate, or wiring is needed. The breakthroughs needed were in ideas, in the ability to foresee groundswells of needs, in the recognition of values, personally and professionally. Jerry Yang and David Filo started Yahoo as a compilation of interesting websites to share with their friends. The service grew into the most visited destination on the Internet at the time, as Yang and Filo were there proprietors of the treasure map of the new land. Yahoo became the standard in "navigation service" in the digital landscape.[59]

New types of services proliferated, as the virtualizing of services became the strategy of greatest ease and highest returns. E-tailers popped up in droves. Stock trading services such as Ameritrade and E*Trade innovated and navigated regulatory channels to provide Internet users the ability to trade stocks from the comfort of their homes. Today there are numerous services that result from the virtualizing of everything from fitness and dieting to meetings, conferences, and gambling.

Viewing their businesses within ecosystems allow digital service companies to leverage the span, density, interactions, and value exchanges of enormous networks consisting of

[59] **Yahoo! Media Relations.** The History of Yahoo! - How It All Started... *Yahoo Media Relations Home.* [Online] 2005. [Cited: May 31, 2011.] http://docs.yahoo.com/info/misc/history.html.

thousands and millions of participants of various types. It allows them to understand the power of aggregating and transforming capitals to align with the capital needs of additional types of participants. For example, aggregating the eyeballs of millions of customers enables the transformation of traffic to financial capital to defray the costs of services from suppliers, making services free or very inexpensive. This has the effect of further increasing adoption and acceptance, which in return provides the basis for more traffic. Virtualization and the ecosystem viewed together enable this recognition of opportunities. Traditional businesses, when grown to certain scale (e.g., franchises), can just as effectively utilize the ecosystem concept to recognize opportunities born out of large numbers and interconnections.

An interesting example can be seen with the current king of search, Google. As a service that serves up billions of searches a day, the opportunities that exist for Google with its massive numbers are numerous, from directing traffic for revenue (which it has taken advantage of via AdWords) to cross-selling online data-storage to office software over the Internet to travel searches. With each opportunity comes a new set of participants in the ecosystem and new scenarios of sustainability and alignment to explore. Amazon recently offered free online storage to customers to stimulate demand for its products and services in a strategy that can be understood by looking at its ecosystem.[60]

Virtual services also depend on the ability to virtualize certain offline components. Online education must adequately replicate the participatory nature of a class room. Online meetings must allow for white-boarding and speaker interruption. LegalZoom, for example, must be able to navigate the different state laws as well as signature requirements of legal forms and the licensing of its advice. Profounder, a new entrant in the crowdfunding space, spent a significant amount of time to navigate the regulatory processes of fund-raising prior to launching its service. Last but not least, PayPal, as an online payment service, must ensure the security of its transactions in addition to providing for fraud protection and identity and business type verification. The creativity and ingenuity of Internet entrepreneurs in devising online procedures that adequately satisfy as replacement of age-old offline procedures reward them with a large and global market that transacts 24 hours a day, 7 days a week. The mix

---

[60] **Davis, Don.** Amazon offers free online storage and streaming of music and video. *Internet Retailer.* March 29, 2011.

of online and offline procedures (e.g., to open an account with E*Trade, a signature is required and funding must occur, thus incurring certain offline latency) mean a more complex ecosystem to coordinate and from which to capture capitals. Understanding clearly the ecosystem and its participants is critical to the sustainability and success of businesses that depends on the digital service strategy.

Intermediary Strategies

Intermediary strategies include both those employed by infomediaries and exchanges. We previously discussed Xignite as an infomediary. Many exchanges exist and act as a matching service for demand and supply. Some go further to stimulate demand and/or supply. eHarmony and Match.com web-based dating services employ techniques to grow membership which increase both supply and demand. The most successful example of this strategy, however, is eBay. By increasing membership, the service increases not only supply but demand. Even better, the increase in membership also leverages network effects. The primary ecosystem is much easier to manage and sustain for matching services, as the key participants are the demand and supply, in addition to the services themselves. This allows the services to focus on value capture, aggregation, and transformation. The services can also employ catalysts acting as partners to reduce friction in payment, in interaction (e.g., increasing trust such as eBay's merchant ratings), and in referrals.

Platform Strategies

Service companies tend to extend their ecosystems to become platforms as this is a natural outgrowth of the size and numbers they achieve. Platform companies have even more opportunities to capture, aggregate, and transform capitals than plumbing or infrastructure companies. They have more capabilities to differentiate their products through the structuring of their platforms. We previously mentioned Amazon moving into online storage. Even before this move, Amazon has already been operating data centers for rent by software and Internet companies. Its popular EC2 product services the who's who of Internet companies.[61] Even plumbing and access companies can extend their ecosystems to services and platforms via the opportunities in numbers and scalability of virtual products. Apple is a well-known example. Apple has vertically integrated from plumbing and access (i.e.,

---

[61] **Wikipedia.** Amazon Web Services - Wikipedia. *Wikipedia.* [Online] May 4, 2011. [Cited: May 31, 2011.] http://en.wikipedia.org/wiki/Amazon_Web_Services.

making computers and software, iPod, iPhone, and iPad) to platforms (i.e., iTunes, App Store). By going beyond providing connections in the ecosystem to capturing part of each piece of value being exchanged between developers and users, Apple can aggregate capitals to the tune of billions of dollars, making it the world's most valuable technology company.

Salesforce.com began as a software service and has evolved into a software platform. Its Force.com platform competes with Amazon in delivering a cloud computing platform. However, Salesforce.com focus is in the enterprise software market, promising to disrupt the traditional enterprise software industry long dominated by Oracle, SAP, and Microsoft.[62]

Analytics and Long Tail Strategies

As platforms and services mature and their particular mixes of services and participants are better known, their ecosystems allow for a strategy that specifically depends on the different capital requirements of different participant types. Services such as Google and LinkedIn, by understanding the needs and types of capitals required by different participants, can afford

---

[62] **Salesforce.com.** Force.com. *Salesforce.com.* [Online] April 2011.

to charge (or acquire financial capital) more from certain types of participants than others. For example, Google charges more for popular AdWords, leveraging its round-trip analytics, and monetizes based on "long tails" by selling AdWords that are less common but nonetheless valuable to particular merchants. LinkedIn identified different groups of users and charge some while providing free service to others.

The strategy depends on an understanding of the degrees of needs of different participant types. To pinpoint the correct constituents for different price levels or pricing structures requires analytics that can tease out characteristics impactful to perceived values and willingness to pay. A "long tail" strategy requires a comprehensive yet detailed dataset in order to follow and serve the "tail." Both strategies require experimentation and fine-tuning for data collection and adjustments in order to achieve sustainability. Ingeniously, Google lets its users perform its experiment through their own devices by letting them bid on AdWords.

Community Strategies

Even though the community strategy emerged during the dotcom bubble, its ecosystem was not sustainable. At the time the member participants and the supplier participants experienced net capital gain, through community services and equipment, bandwidth, and software sales, respectively the community operators were experiencing net capital loss because they were not charging the member participants the requisite membership dues required to offset infrastructure and operating costs.

Many communities were presuming the endless source of revenue of advertising, but neither their membership numbers nor the adoption of online advertising was far enough along to support their assumptions. One of the key lessons of the dotcom burst was that advertising cannot be counted on as the primary source of revenue. But even this lesson's usefulness wore down in the years that followed as operating costs for online communities decreased and advertising revenues increased.

Community allows business to stay closer to their customers. Even more powerfully, communities provide closed value systems. They have lots of data points and can monitor conversations and potentially recognize every interaction, conversation, and value exchange. In practical business activities, it is no longer enough to be just a service or a platform, one needs community for product feedback, product launch, announcements, and ideas (e.g., t-shirt design crowdsourcing).

Quite a few emerging companies are dedicated to helping businesses build communities. CommunitySpark, CommuniSpace, GetSatisfaction, and KickApps are a few examples.

Advertising Strategies

The second iteration of communities saw membership numbers on massive scales, in the hundreds of millions, while, at the same time, operating and bandwidth costs decreased dramatically. These two factors make advertising a viable strategy for digital companies. Proofs arrive in the form of PlentyOfFish, Facebook, and Myspace. The original assumption of viability for businesses based on advertising was correct after all. The assumption was incorrect (during the dotcom bubble) in the "escape-velocity" numbers needed to support the ecosystems of communities at the time.

Crowdsourcing Strategies

The massive number of members in communities and on platforms enables another strategic phenomenon, that of crowdsourcing. Crowdsourcing and social network strategies aim to harness the power of crowds of members by directing their online activities to useful but fun and satisfying tasks. Examples include t-shirt design in the community Threadless[63] and, of course, Wikipedia itself. Though there are some differences noted, the open-source software movement can be considered a type of crowdsourcing, albeit the number of participants involved in open-source is smaller and the level of coordination required for open-source is more complex.

Viewed in terms of an ecosystem, crowdsourcing makes tremendous sense, as values created by member participants are captured, aggregated, and transformed into capitals that not only support the costs of the platform and/or community, there is also room for rewards and credit-claiming. Crowdsourcing would not be viable without capital aggregation.

[63] **Wikipedia.** Wikipedia. *Wikipedia.* [Online] May 7, 2011. [Cited: May 31, 2011.] http://en.wikipedia.org/wiki/Threadless.

Crowdfunding Strategies

Crowdfunding taps into the power of capital aggregation by accumulating pledges of numerous members who are supportive of the same projects. Some well-known crowdfunding companies are Kickstarter and Profounder. One of the key innovations of crowdfunding is the stipulation that if the project does not reach its funding goal within a certain timeframe, all commitment of supporting funds up to that point are rolled back. This stipulation communicates to the supporters that the project will only be funded and go forward if there is enough of a groundswell of support. The social validation capital it provides the supporter, though not critical, creates a certain level of social security (or social proof) to catalyze pledging. It also communicates to the initiator of the project the validation of his or her idea, should the project reaches its funding goal in the allotted time.

This innovation in the crowdfunding strategy effectively captures the value of support, aggregates that value and transforms it into either the financial capital that the project initiator sought or the information capital that will help her refine her ideas and, at the same time, help the pledgers compare their thinking and support with each other. This very innovation of capturing and aggregating intention value is taken up one more notch in the strategy of group buying business models such as Groupon and Living Social.

Social Bookmarking Strategies

Social bookmarking is a direct descendant of crowdsourcing, harnessing the power of crowds to tag web sites and pages and share those tags with others. Some of the more popular companies employing this strategy are Digg, Reddit, Mixx, StumbleUpon, and del.icio.us.

The ecosystem of social bookmarking is noteworthy in at least one aspect: the instant exchange of information capital among participants. One member can tag sites that he sees and, at the same time view sites tagged by other members. This allows for a sort of interactive build-up of tagging, making for dynamic value creation and aggregation. Besides the obvious information capital that the network gains and distributes to its participants, the social and emotional satisfaction of contributing to a community, as well as the intellectual capital of surveying and marking information, helps create engagement among the participants. To transform the capitals captured and aggregated thus far to financial capital will require a level of aggregation and organization of information capital that is currently not available in the present crop of sites.

Social Network Strategies

While crowdsourcing strategies take advantage of the massive number of connections one has, social network strategies and viral loops take advantage of the massive number of connections that one's connections have. We discuss crowdsourcing and social network separately, but in reality many implemented strategies blend both as they are born out of the same phenomenon - the laws of massive numbers. Whereas in crowdsourcing, the crowd is solicited for its work or wisdom on a particular topic, in social networks, it is leveraged for its connections and its ability to communicate and relay messages via connections. A social network can be employed purely to propagate a message or to perform actual tasks and provide judgment. Just as there are social network strategies that employ crowdsourcing, there are crowdsourcing strategies that employ social networks.

Social networks are very popular currently. The most well-known, of course, is Facebook, but Meetup, Myspace, Orkut,

Bebo, and LinkedIn are also highly successful social networks. These networks have members in the hundreds of millions.

Because social networks are relatively "closed" environments, i.e., once a user enters Facebook, most of her activities are contained within Facebook, the potential to capture capitals is enormous. Very few value leaks can occur if the social network does not allow them.

Because of their large membership and span and density, social networks make ideal platform for the implementation of other services, such as games, messaging, and multiple types of interactions ranging from photo sharing to event planning, spurring a massive number of developers to deploy applications on them, ever-enlarging the ecosystem of the social network. Because they are closed platforms, social networks have the power to monetize capital exchanges that occur, even those triggered and conducted by third parties deploying their services on the platform. Additionally the closed platform allows a social network to mine the characteristics and interactions of its members for targeting and marketing purposes, stoking the stratospheric valuations. Lastly the well-known network effects contribute to the increases in size of social networks as everyone wants to be where their friends are. There would not be much value to be "linked in" into a network of only a dozen people. Even if one never ends up interacting with the other 100 million members in the network, knowing that there is a path from where he is to any of those members increases the perceived value of the network in his mind.

The ecosystem of a social network is undoubtedly complex, as numerous types of participants exist, emerge, and evolve. The success of these ecosystems depends largely on their ability to align the participants for capital exchanges, capture, aggregation, and transformation, without infringing upon their interactions and privacy. Facebook has launched multiple attempts to effect alignment among its participant types. Some efforts succeeded, and some failed miserably, even causing backlash from the community. One such failed effort is the Beacon feature. The Likes feature has been able to gain traction and helps Facebook align its members' preferences with the values needed by businesses and advertisers.

Another example of efforts at aligning participants in an ecosystem is Meetup's Perks feature. It is Meetup's effort in aligning the advertising capital needed by its client companies with the values of the various Meetup groups. The program's success or failure is difficult to gauge at this point, but its success will largely hinge on Meetup's ability to align specific reciprocal capitals in exchanges between two of its key participant types: the sponsors and the group organizers (as well as their members).

Viral Strategies

Adam Penenberg, a professor at NYU Stern School of Business, wrote the very insightful and fascinating book *Viral Loop* in 2009, chronicling the emergence of what he calls "viral loop" companies.[64] From Hot or Not to Flickr to Ning to Facebook, Penenberg assesses the significance of the viral propagation within a social network, and even went so far as to provide formulas for calculating viral growth metrics.

What makes a concept viral cannot be summed up in a formula, as it involves psychology, tastes, influences, and other social characteristics, but within the framework of an ecosystem, "virality" is a catalyst that can provide transition of states for a network toward targeted span, density, and interactions. One can calculate the propagation speed of a network assuming certain level of friction between nodes and

[64] **Penenberg, Adam.** *Viral Loop.* New York : Hyperion, 2009.

connections, but the mechanism for "virality" hinges on the need for one node to relay the message that it received. The motivation could be social proof, horde behavior, sense of sharing, or a digital version of an extroverted personality. Certainly, this is an area begging for experimentation and adjustment in the digital realm, just like any other formulation of state transition catalysts.

Viral loops, as Penenberg refers to them, are incredibly powerful mechanisms to increase the value potential within the ecosystem as we frame it. They also offer a new level of complexity in the ecosystem by introducing new categorization of participants such as influencers or connectors, mavens, and salesmen, per Malcolm Gladwell's eloquent naming.[65] Capital ecosystems must be structured to align the capital exchanges between these participant types and the producers of the messages.

Numerous services and businesses have emerged to provide techniques and tactics for catalyzing state transitions a social network. They range from GetGlue to CloudSponge. Some services even focus on the characteristics of particular types of participants, e.g., Klout.com. In actuality, they measure

[65] **Gladwell, Malcolm.** *The Tipping Point: How Little Things Can Make....* s.l. : Back Bay Books, 2002.

participants' relational capital and help them transform it to other types of capital. These services are prime examples of the ecosystems our framework explores.

Mobile Strategies

With the advent of smart phones and the embedment of GPS receivers in mobile phones as required by the FCC, the mobile strategy taps into a new massive base of users on the move.[66] Because access is even more ubiquitous, businesses that provide real-time services stand to gain the most. Research in Motion (RIM) became a darling for its mobile devices that provide email access. Social networks such as Facebook and LinkedIn gain even more traction as users constantly check the streams of postings from their friends and associates. A major participant type in the mobile ecosystem is the mobile application developer. The more mobile access users have to the digital world, the more opportunities to provide services that are not necessarily business oriented or professionally required, but rather life-enhancing. Games have become a major force in the mobile application marketplace, as have photo, music, and video sharing applications and services.

---

[66] *GPS Is Smartening Up Your Cell Phone.* **Charles, Dan.** 2006, NPR.

Apple became a huge beneficiary via its iTunes Store, justifying its effort in creating the ecosystem for its devices such as iPod, iPhone, and iPad. Applications on mobile devices continue to proliferate, satisfying the demand of users who have access to the digital landscape almost every second of their day. As more applications become available, the base of users in turn grow since the variety of applications allows the mobile platform to satisfy almost every need, whim, and fancy. IDC expects the number of smart phones shipped in 2011 to rise to 472 million from 305 million in 2010.[67] This upward spiral continues.

Location-Based Services Strategies

One of the most interesting intersections of strategies occurs when mobile services connect with location-based services (LBS). The users are now tethered to the digital realm even geographically, so that in effect he is always on the grid, as knowing his physical location allows the grid to virtually engulf him. Navigation services ensue and became indispensible. Location awareness now enables the users to connect to his locale in a way impossible with his natural five senses. The

[67] **IDC.** IDC Press Release - prUS22871611. *IDC.* [Online] June 9, 2011. [Cited: June 9, 2011.] http://www.idc.com/getdoc.jsp?containerId=prUS22871611.

user now has a sixth sense, the digital sense. And as long as the world around him checks in digitally and exists on the grid, he is completely aware of it, so that nearby restaurants offering his favorite foods pop up in his consciousness via his cell phone as he enters the vicinity.

By registering activities in the real world onto the digital grid, Foursquare creates a capital ecosystem that sustains the capital gains for users, merchants, and itself. Foursquare implements a number of strategies in concert: LBS, mash-up, and games. By encouraging members to register themselves at locations to earn points, it provides elements of a game to the activities of the participants. By mashing up the real, physical locations of members (via LBS) with the virtual map of merchants in a locale, Foursquare can encourage activities in certain locales.[68] In the context of our capital exchange framework, Foursquare uses the combined strategies to align the participant types in its ecosystem for reciprocal sustaining capital exchanges.

Mash-ups Strategies

Though we have described Foursquare's employment of the mash-up strategy to encourage activities in physical locations,

[68] **Wikipedia.** foursquare (social network) - Wikipedia. *Wikipedia.* [Online] May 25, 2011. [Cited: May 31, 2011.] http://en.wikipedia.org/wiki/Foursquare_(social_network).

mash-up represents a strategy with broader implications when any type of service is "mashed up" with another type of service. The most popular type of mash-up has been to superimpose information or service on top of a physical locale via a map. But mash-up can also be done on the time dimension, as when events are plotted against a timeline. We can say that we have mashed up our description of digital strategies with time as we discuss the evolution of digital strategies. Mash-ups in general can catalyze activities by putting together phenomena that don't typically occur together, creating interesting possibilities. They encourage creative connections via additional dimensions by connecting concepts that begin with one or more dimensions in common, introducing into the creative conscious relevant information not yet included. In our framework, they can help align the capital exchanges of participant types in an ecosystem, as Foursquare illustrates.

Augmented Reality Strategies

When virtual reality or information is mashed up against physical reality, augmented reality results. Games have emerged where players in real, physical locations take on roles that are provided to them via a digital reality, allowing physical space to serve as nothing more than a mechanism for visceral feel and touch validating a digital plan or strategy. In other words, where traditionally the conventions and constraints of the physical world ultimately determine the outcomes of activities, now virtual conventions and constraints can be imposed on the actions in the physical world (of course, with all parties agreeing and subscribing to the rules), allowing for infinitely more variety in interactions. Augmented reality, as a type of mash-up strategy, also allows for the alignment of capital exchanges to facilitate an ecosystem's sustainability and optimality.

Games Strategies

A natural by-product of augmented reality is the application to games, especially now that players can be constantly connected to the digital plain. But game strategies can have wider implications to an ecosystem, especially within the confines of a community such as Facebook. Farmville, for example, allows Facebook friends to build a farm together.[69] Games not only serve as entertainment but can also help align the interests and interactions of participants in a community. Other games

---

[69] **Wire, Business.** *Zynga's FarmVille Becomes Largest and Fastest Growing Social Game Ever.* s.l. : Business Wire, 2009.

involve ways for participants to acquire points within a community in the same way that contributors to a website are awarded points. Many sites have started implementing games to incentivize users toward certain behavior. Examples include Perks on Meetup and BuxBack on Mojopages. Another example is ScratchBack, which is described as a virtual tip jar that also links back to the tipper's page.[70] In the context of our capital exchange framework, ScratchBack strategy helps ensure reciprocal value exchange at the transaction level.

The figure below provides a visual lineage of digital strategies from 1944 (when the first computer, the ENIAC, was developed) to 2011. The lineage map also details the technologies enabling the strategies, as well as some of the companies that successfully leveraged them.

---

[70] **Scratchback.** Scratchback FAQ's. *Scratchback.* [Online] 2011. http://www.scratchback.com/.

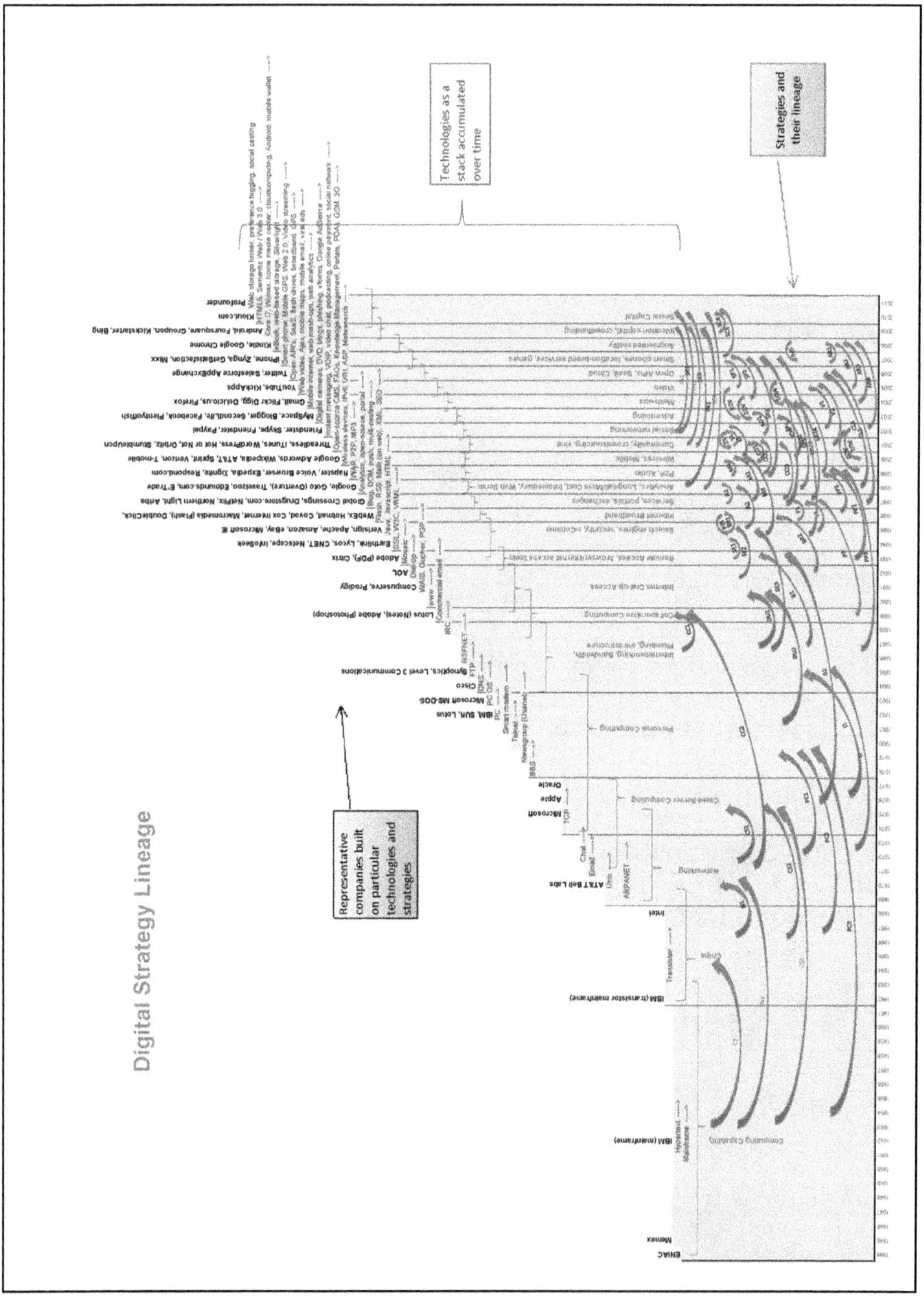

Figure 9 - Digital Strategy Timeline with Supporting Technologies and Representative Companies

Strategy Lineage, Layers and Sets

Many businesses employ multiple strategies. However, when employing multiple strategies, the companies must be sure that the strategies are aligned and, at the very least, do not conflict. Ideally the strategies should be layered in such a way that they align, support, complement, and leverage each other.

Key to strategy alignment is the understanding of strategy lineage, within one's industry and within one's own ecosystem. For example, in the Internet industry, why does platform follow services and infrastructure? Why does community follow platform? Understanding the strategy lineage provides insights into the evolution of values and their exchange, capture, and transformation. Invariably, if one strategy dominates, it is because that strategy either provides additional or more important values, or it is better at controlling the ecosystem's capital structure. For instance, many Internet destinations have begun adding videos, quick user-feedback mechanisms, and even game-playing features to provide additional values that their users desire, as sites compete on more than just the original intrinsic values they provide. Technologies have also moved from increasing span and density of networks to catalyzing interactions, capital exchanges, capital capture, aggregation, storage, and transformation.

Understanding strategy lineage helps one evolve his or her capital ecosystem to take advantage of technologies, processes, and practices that capture, aggregate, and make use of additional values. We thus propose an approach to construct the strategy set that follows the sustainable progression of activities to assert control over the ecosystem's capital structure. The approach also blends strategies discussed to the progression of capture structure control, taking advantage of both proven and emerging capabilities of technologies to substantiate the strategies and the capture structure.

Let us examine some demonstrated examples of capital structure control by some of the strategies discussed.

Value Capture

We previously mention Klout.com as a service that perfectly illustrates the need to capture, aggregate, and convert capital within an ecosystem.[71] Value capture strategies is one of the key ways to generate enormous wealth and capital from a

---

[71] **TechCrunch.** Klout - Crunchbase Profile. *Crunchbase.* [Online] May 29, 2011. [Cited: May 31, 2011.] http://www.crunchbase.com/company/klout.

large-span and highly dense network with many interactions. Inevitably through interactions, capitals are exchanged, and many are captured, but many can also dissipate. A restaurant that does not ask its customer to provide feedback forgoes an enormous amount of information capital and possibly brand, satisfaction, loyalty, and relational capital. Yelp and Mojopages help business capture these capitals through user ratings and feedback.[72]

Value capture also includes value identification, as identification is a necessary part of capture. OpenTable identifies the value of restaurant goers' intention and captures it as soon as these participants realize the need for a venue. OpenTable captures the value in the form of reservations which it then packages and sells to restaurants in the form of reservations made and customers seated. OpenTable's ecosystem includes not only the patrons but also the restaurant venues, related services, and the casual users of the system who are its prospective members and source of capitals.[73]

OpenTable's ecosystem is vulnerable because, with no pun intended, it is rather open. The platform, unlike Facebook,

---

[72] —. Mojopages - Crunchbase Profile. *Crunchbase*. [Online] October 15, 2010. [Cited: May 31, 2011.] http://www.crunchbase.com/company/mojopages.

[73] **Hafner, Katie.** Restaurant Reservations Go Online . *New York Times*. June 18, 2007.

does not lock in the participants, allowing OpenTable only a tenuous connection with participants via an email. Patrons can make reservations but decide not to honor them, choosing to directly reserve with the restaurants. OpenTable and the restaurants (to the degree that they agree to align with OpenTable) can discourage no-shows by remembering the customers via their emails and names, but the stick is not big enough, as restaurants would not willingly turn away a customer even if that customer has a history of no-shows. One could argue that Groupon's ecosystem has the same vulnerability. However, the stick Groupon carries is rather "bigger" than the one OpenTable possesses. Once a patron participates in a Groupon deal, he has committed his credit card and is financially accountable to the deal once it materializes. The financial commitment with credit card information provides Groupon additional deterrence against "no-shows".

Capital Transformation

Capital transformation is amply demonstrated by OpenTable transforming its reservations to financial capital, by Klout.com transforming its users' influence capital to real-world perks and rewards, and by 7-Eleven transforming its logistics to convenience and finally to financial capital. There are more intricacies involved in capital transformation, however.

Many transformations of capitals require a critical threshold level of source capital. For example, a website needs a minimal number of click-throughs before it can convert them to advertising revenue, as every blogger can relate. OpenTable cannot convert the reservation capital to financial capital unless it provides enough reservations to the restaurant to make it worthwhile for the restaurant. Most poignantly, Groupon cannot convert the buying commitment capital of groups of buyers to financial capital for itself without meeting the minimum number of buyers for the deals. It cannot turn relational capital (in the form of customers on its mailing list) into financial capital (in the form of revenue from the merchants) without a critical threshold number of members to create liquidity for its deals.

Beyond meeting the required threshold for transformation, capital transformations give rise to transformation factors, a measure of the efficiency of transformation. It is akin to the conversion rates between currencies. Similar to currency exchange rates, capital transformation factors can fluctuate. A simple observation will illustrate: in bad economic times, salaries are depressed, making the transformation rate of human capital to financial capital is very low. This explains why in recessions, many go back to school to stock up on their intellectual capital. Then, in boom times, when salaries are high, their intellectual capital, which has been accumulated, can be exchanged back to financial capital in higher amounts and at higher rates.

Capital transformation rates can be drastically altered by technology. Technologies can therefore disrupt the transformations that occur in an ecosystem, destroying incumbent capital exchanges, altering some exchanges, and creating other exchanges. These disruptions can completely revise the sustainability of the ecosystem, thereby creating entirely new ecosystems. Witness the demise of the newspaper industry because of online advertising and sites like Craigslist.org.[74]

Previously we examined the models and ecosystems of well-established and successful businesses. We can use the same capital sustainability framework to analyze interesting up-and-comers that utilize novel and innovative strategies to achieve the same characteristics of size, density, interactions, value

---

[74] **Hau, Louis.** Newspaper Killer. *Forbes Magazine.* December 11, 2006.

exchange, value aggregation, and value transformation. The framework can help us analyze their business models, gain a deep understanding of their value creation mechanisms, and assess their growth potential. Below is a representative list of these up-and-comers.

Table 1 – Some Digital Up-and-Comers

Company	Type
AirBnB	Air and Bed & Breakfast Booking
CloudSponge	Social Networking
Diaspora	Distributed Social Networking
Dropbox	Cloud Storage
FourSquare	Augmented Reality
GoldSpot Media	Video Advertising
Klout.com	Social Capital
Last FM	Internet Radio
Plentyoffish	Internet Dating
Profounder	Crowdfunding
Quora	Knowledge Management Analytics
Scribd	Digital Publishing
Slideshare	Publication Tool
SocialGuide	Social TV Guide
Spotify	Mass Customized Music
Square	Mobile Payment
Vator.tv	Entrepreneur Community
Yelp	Local Merchant Reviews & Listing
Zinga	Social Games

Chapter

7

> "Human subtlety will never devise an invention more beautiful, more simple or more direct than does nature because in her inventions nothing is lacking, and nothing is superfluous."
>
> -Leonardo da Vinci

7. Inventing an Ecosystem

Recall our discussion of the potential value of a capital ecosystem as identified by the following attributes:

- Span
- Density
- Interactions and Capital Exchanges
- Capital Alignment
- Capital Capture
- Capital Aggregation
- Capital Transformation

Some of the attributes are necessary for sustainability, e.g., density and exchanges. Others are preferable but not necessary, e.g., alignment, aggregation, and transformation.

A capital ecosystem can be sustainable simply with critical density and exchanges. Without critical density, there will not be enough interactions. And without enough interactions, there will not be an adequate level of value exchanges to justify the net value gained by each participant to ensure the participant's continued participation.

With alignment, the ecosystem can be even more effective at creating value, as multiple events and transitions reinforce each other's effects, amplifying the capitals exchanged and gained by the involved participants, e.g., the customer is also a partner and a marketer.

With aggregation, minute values that appear meaningless with a single occurrence take on significance, even disruptive power, when large numbers of instances are gathered and accumulated. Giving someone directions to a hardware store seems helpful but financially insignificant, since one receives no compensation for such an act. However, being able to say to the hardware store that one has directed 100,000 potential customers to the store and know that approximately 0.1% of these individuals end up purchasing something at the store, one can negotiate a referral commission with the store. This is what Google and Internet advertising systems are able to do.

Converting Internet traffic to ad dollars is an obvious and prevalent example of capital transformation. A less obvious example includes the concept of crowdsourcing, using the large number of members or users to gather information, ideas, designs and concepts. Still another non-obvious example is the transformation of information capital to marketing capital in order to target segments of customers willing to pay, helping to fund the operations for the whole service. LinkedIn utilizes this transformation to target recruiters and premium service users in order to obtain revenue that operates the whole site. This is a result of the understanding gained through customer analytics. Google operates an ecosystem that includes merchants who bid on AdWords, leveraging both analytics and the phenomenon of "long-tail" marketing that Chris Anderson wrote about.[75] These two strategies are enabled by the information capital

---

[75] **Anderson, Chris.** *The Long Tail: Why the Future of Business is Selling Less of More.* New York : Hyperion, 2006.

that Google received from other participants in its ecosystem. One of the most subtle examples of capital transformation is 7-Eleven's conversion of logistics and retailing site presence to convenience capital and then to financial capital by charging customers a premium on its items.

Value capture seems obvious, yet its subtle effects in the new economy can be enormous. It is the main reason behind the meteoric valuation of Facebook. In a classical transaction, payment is collected after a sale, and payment occurs through a financial clearing channel such as the act of handing over the dollar bills, the sending of a check, or the provision of credit card information. These channels for currency, or financial capital movements, have evolved over centuries and decades, and the platform for the capture of financial capital is well established, with checks and balances. With the digital economy, numerous different types of capitals exist. Whoever is able to construct a platform to capture these rather ethereal capitals will stand to gain tremendously. Facebook, being a platform that captures all interactions of its members, is able to capture any capitals created within that environment (including conversational capitals, especially), whereas Google is only able to capture search traffic, as the traffic moves past Google onto other web destinations. Google successfully enlarged its ecosystem by purchasing DoubleClick in 2007 for $3.1 billion, giving it access to banner ad real estate across the web, but it still cannot approach the kind of closed-system capital capture of which Facebook is capable.[76]

After capture, all capitals, whether financial, tangible (e.g., machines, buildings), or brand (e.g., word-of-mouth, mindshare) have shelf life. Some capitals significantly decrease with time (e.g., news, information capital); some dissipate much more slowly (e.g., real estate). Business should create and employ repositories for capitals that keeps their values "fresh" longer and implement tactics to guard against activities that can decay their values, whether the capitals involve fresh produce or customer loyalty. The repository also provides a ready supply of capitals for transformation to different capitals as needed.

The innovative business model that combines capital capture, aggregation and conversion in a capital-aligned ecosystem that

---

[76] **Story, Louise and Helft, Miguel.** Google Buys DoubleClick for $3.1 Billion. *The New York Times.* April 14, 2007.

has achieved critical density and capital exchanges through interactions has enormous potential. Witness Facebook, Netflix, and LinkedIn.

The Mini Field Guide

In the previous chapter, we surveyed the various strategies employed to create value by digital companies both well-known and emerging. We examined these strategies against an informal timeline of the development of the digital economy, as well as in the context of our capital ecosystem framework and its value potential assessment. We now present a condensed guide to creating innovative and viable businesses with supporting sustainable capital ecosystems, making use of both our framework and the strategies that we have discussed.

This is a condensed guide, since the full reference includes detailed descriptions, examples and modeling explanations, extending beyond the scope of this book.

1. Start Simple

   A viable business model can simply start with a description of the service or product provided to fulfill an existing need, whether or not that need is currently met by other businesses. Identifying and fulfilling an unmet need is obviously an advantage, but perhaps even with needs that are already met, the new business idea involves a more cost-effective or higher-quality product or service. More importantly the idea should recognize capitals currently desired by the target consumer, but not identified, provided, captured, aggregated, and/or transformed to satisfy that consumer. The supporting description of the target consumer may be a natural development of the description of the capitals desired in the exchange, and the final description may include the details of the environment and the context in which the capital exchanges take place. We term this description the capital scenario.

If this initial capital ecosystem of just the provider and consumer of desired capitals shows a new product or service at a better price, with higher quality and/or better customer service than currently available, then all that is left is to prove are assumptions and calculations for a business plan.

Two possibilities then exist.

If the model is correct, focus should then shift to execution.

If the model is incorrect, e.g., perhaps the cost assumptions are wrong and the customers' willingness to pay is lower than anticipated, then the next steps are to explore the business model through the capital sustainability framework thus far presented. The next steps are:

2. List all interactions between the current participants.

3. Identify all possible capitals and capital exchanges between the current participants.

4. Identify capital exchanges that currently exist.

5. Identify all capital exchanges that should exist, and provide explanations as to why they are not currently happening. For each of those capital exchanges, ask the following questions:

   - Is it because one party in the exchange does not see net capital gain?

- Is it because neither party in the exchange sees net capital gain?

6. Ask the following questions regarding the capitals in the capital exchanges that should exist to make the transactions profitable to both parties:

    a. Do these capitals currently exist in the ecosystem?

    b. Are these capitals currently captured?

    c. Do any of these capitals only acquire significance in large numbers?

    d. If so, are these capitals aggregated? Can they be? If so, how?

    e. Are these capitals currently stored somewhere as they are aggregated, or do they dissipate instantly?

    f. Can these capitals be converted to capitals that dissipate less quickly?

    g. What currently available platforms, infrastructures, software, technologies, processes, and/or techniques exist to help capture, aggregate, store, and convert the capitals that occur in the exchanges that should exist to make participation in the capital ecosystem viable for each participant?

7. Create a model that accounts for these capitals and their anticipated exchanges to determine the sustainability of the ecosystem, given the exploration of strategies, technologies and platforms to manage the capitals.

8. If the model does not bear out the sustainability of the ecosystem, is it possible that the ecosystem needs to include an additional participant?

9. If an additional participant can be identified, reevaluate the ecosystem by going back through steps 2 to 8.

Toward Sustainability

One can adapt a capital ecosystem to achieve sustainability by doing the following:

- Increase density – by adding participants or layers of participants and creating connections

- Increase exchanges – by triggering interactions

- Achieve alignment – by sequencing and leveraging transitions involving similar capital exchanges

- Achieve additional net capital – by developing new capitals and new capital transformations, by selecting platforms that can better capture, aggregate, and store capitals or by expanding the current platform

Multiple Ecosystems

Some businesses, whether due to size or technical constraints, participate in multiple ecosystems. For these businesses, aligning, and, if possible, integrating the ecosystems, may prove to be of great value. A customer in one ecosystem may exist as a competitor in another. Having both in the same ecosystem allows the business to balance the capital exchanges with that business. A partner in one ecosystem may become a customer in another ecosystem. Cooperation with the partner takes on higher importance as its value as a customer in the second ecosystem is recognized. Most often, a customer in one ecosystem will turn out to be also a customer in another ecosystem.   Opportunities to develop loyalty with the customer will then exist at multiple touch-points.

Though specifics on alignment and integration of multiple ecosystems are beyond the scope of this book, we can note that the basic approach is to map out the separate ecosystems and link them via the participants that the ecosystems have in common.

> "Don't reinvent the wheel, just realign it."
>
> -Anthony J. D'Angelo

8. Re-Invention

I f the central theme of our story has been capital transformation, then the characters are the participants, and the capital ecosystem is the setting. Every business - digital, hybrid, or traditional - can re-invent itself along with its capital ecosystem to leverage the power of the connected economy, even though digital businesses are able to exercise more influence within shorter timeframes on their ecosystems since their activities are almost always captured.

Because every business has networks or groups in which it participates, an imperative for every business is to identify all of its networks. The business can then re-invent its own ecosystem by integrating and aligning these groups. The values that the business creates and exchanges in one network can be reused, leveraged, accumulated, and amplified in all others. An overall capital ecosystem for the business should be constructed to comprehensively understand, systematize, and quantify the business's value footprints and to tune the business model for sustainability and adaptability through innovations. The business's ecosystem should be evaluated according to Step 7 from the prior chapter to determine sustainability. If sustainability does not exist, Steps 8 and 9 should be followed.

Very simple networks currently exist for many businesses but are more than likely disconnected. Take the customer mailing list or the prospect list. This is the group the business has created with its potential customers. Take also the Facebook Friends and Like lists and the LinkedIn Connections. Are all three groups synchronized and harmonized into an ecosystem? What are the participant types in the ecosystem? What capitals is the business currently exchanging with them?

Community is the top layer of an ecosystem, consisting of all participants with their respective groups. A community can be built in many ways, but one of the most effective, if not the most effective, ways is to develop connections, interactions, and capital exchanges, because value creation within the ecosystem evolve from the interactions. Software and services, both commercial and open-source, now exist to create communities for a business or its products. Acquia, built on the popular Drupal content management system (CMS), is one such software.[77]

Interactions within a community, however, are normally supported by a platform whether it is a mall, the US postal mail system, the telephone network, the Internet, the mobile devices, or a combination of these channels. Now, more than ever, platforms exist to create, develop, fine-tune, and leverage capital ecosystems. No longer will it take days to call every customer or to send them thank-you cards just to keep the business's presence in their minds. An email to a list of thousands or even millions takes no more than a few minutes, even with embedded multimedia. The traditional thank-you cards can be efficiently substituted with e-cards. Customers can provide instant feedback via community services such as the aforementioned GetSatisfaction or sites like Yelp and Mojopages.

Paypal provide an effective and efficient platform for financial capital exchange. The capital most supported for exchange is still information. The information exchanged, however, has

[77] **Acquia.** Acquia - About Us. *Acquia is Drupal made Simple | Acquia.* [Online] 2011. [Cited: May 31, 2011.] http://acquia.com/about-us.

evolved. Unstructured, real-time, and interactive information are supported by services like Twitter, Facebook, YouTube, Digg, and StumbleUpon. The marketing message is no longer a one-way push of information toward potential customers. With ad campaign management services, web-based and mobile, customers can be targeted, down to their physical locations, and their responses can be collected in real-time for further refinement of the message. Within a community (i.e., an ecosystem), new product announcements get instant recognition and awareness even before they are available, allowing the business to gauge both enthusiasm and demand. The simple Facebook Like and Google +1 features allow for measurement of potential customer engagement.[78]

Because a community can create a treasure trove of information exchange for a business, the platform or platforms that underlie the community is critical in supporting, promoting, managing, and aggregating the capitals of that community. Many businesses are faced with multiple platforms supporting multiple communities. As the platforms themselves become more and more integrated, the more important focus for the business should be the overarching

---

[78] **Malik, Om.** Google +1, Facebook Likes & the Web Commerce Battle. *Gigaom.* [Online] June 9, 2011. [Cited: June 9, 2011.] http://gigaom.com/2011/06/02/google-1-vs-facebook-likes/.

ecosystem that spans multiple platforms and supports the multiple roles and interactions of the business with all of its customers, suppliers, partners, regulators, and even competitors. Creating an overarching capital ecosystem not only aligns the business's activities for effectiveness and efficiency, but also allows the business to realize resiliency, as inevitably, similar (though not identical) activities are identified and aligned, affording the business the opportunities to more readily recognize "substitute" participants.

Technology is a powerful potential platform disruptor, changing the economics of an ecosystem. Many disruptive technologies get introduced in specific capital ecosystems, as they attack application beach-heads. Having an overarching ecosystem brings the disruptive ecosystem into view and allows for possible diffusion of the technology into all other activities that the business performs. Why should analytics only be applied to website clicks? Why should comments from interested parties be confined only to blogs?

> "We shape our tools and afterwards our tools shape us."
>
> -Marshall McLuhan

9. Tools

The key remaining question at this point is how does one make use of the approach, strategy, and techniques of the framework discussed thus far to invent or reinvent one's capital ecosystem? Numerous tools and services, both online and offline, are now available to help businesses manage, grow, and benefit from their ecosystems. In this chapter, we survey these tools and services and their application to the creation of a vibrant, high-value capital ecosystem.

The Simplest Platform

No doubt many businesses have used their email lists as their de facto digital community platform. Email has primarily been used as a communication platform, and, as such, contributes to the exchange of information capital. The exchange of information capital can lead to gains in relational, intellectual, and financial capital. Though its simplest value proposition is the engagement of participants in the ecosystem, well-utilized communication can create a sense of trust, reliability, responsiveness, and awareness. Email can help validate a connection, signal that your business is open to communication and feedback, encourage further interaction, and opens the door for possible valuable information capital exchange.

As one of the most popular digital platforms, email has grown ubiquitous and become an indispensible business tool. For these reasons, many more advanced tools and services based on the email platform have been developed to help businesses hone and enhance the value of their ecosystem. These include Constant Contact, MailChimp, and Mad Mimi. Within many social network environments, proprietary messaging capabilities are provided to members, providing the in-network mails. These messaging capabilities allow members to communicate with each other, as well as among members and groups of members within the network, allowing for additional connection and interaction density.

With the advent of social networks, various tools have been born to help increase a network's size and density. The well-known LinkedIn site is a key enabler, as is Facebook. Cloudsponge is one such tool, allowing a business's members to invite their friends and associates onto the platform, a function already provided by LinkedIn and Facebook. In promoting its messages, such as product announcements and customer education, businesses can employ the popular tools of Twitter and YouTube. To encourage interaction and community feedback, businesses can employ tools and services such as GetSatisfaction. Events, whether offline or online, can trigger tremendous value exchanges. Evite is a well-known service to plan, organize, communicate, and follow up on events. Eventbrite is another event planning service, but also provides ticketing and promotional capabilities, as does TicketLeap. The exchange of financial capital can be facilitated with well-known services such as PayPal, Amazon Payments, and Google Checkout.

Reaching for Span

The span within a business's ecosystem can be increased with simple activities such as emailing contacts, prospects, customers, and partners to develop and strengthen connections, as well as to include additional participants in the community. Email is an extremely effective medium for both online and traditional businesses to keep in touch. Many tools, including MailChimp and Constant Contact, exist to make this activity even more efficient and effective, by allowing automatic email notifications of events or follow-up communications.

Search engine optimization (SEO) and Google Adwords are effective ways to gather online traffic and enlarge the mindshare of a business. Facebook Likes and Google +1 are two additional ways to develop mindshare by tapping into two of the largest networks on the Internet. Likewise, to achieve mindshare on LinkedIn, not only can a LinkedIn group be created, but also connections can be strengthened by inviting the businesses' contacts to join the LinkedIn group.

Developing Density

Density can be developed either by creating additional one-to-one connections or by creating connections between individuals or groups in your network to other groups and individuals in the network. Density can open up channels of communication and capital exchanges not currently known.

Igniting Interactions

Interactions can be ignited with activities that bring parties together either offline or online. A favorite of offline businesses is the networking mixer to bring members or participants together to meet and mingle with each other. Online, bulletin boards, discussions, and activity streams (similar to Facebook's) can help ignite additional interactions as participants weigh in on subjects of interest to them. Tweets not only provide constant refresh of the connections between a participant and her follower, but can also ignite related discussions. YouTube is a favorite way for companies to introduce and demonstrate their products, and video clips can also be passed on, creating a very effective interaction medium, as the very act of passing on a video is an interaction among participants.

Promoting Value Exchange

Since information is a type of capital, communication itself is a capital exchange. What starts out as an exchange purely of information capital can evolve into intellectual capital exchange and service exchange, perhaps eventually resulting in a reciprocal financial exchange. Facebook's enormous valuation no doubt is fueled by the incredible numbers of interactions occurring between members every second, as everyone's home page is constantly updated with activity feeds from their "friends." The exchange in information can evolve into exchange of other capitals, e.g., virtual gifts sent, invitations to events, recruitment to join in a game, or recommendations to use products or services. By promoting information exchange alone, Facebook is able to identify patterns of preference and customer base characteristics that are invaluable to the transformation of information capital collected to advertising financial capital.

Construct for Capital Capture

We remarked earlier that the ability to capture capitals that thus far have not been captured provide many businesses with enormous opportunities. Many constructs have thus been devised to help capture capitals, especially intangible capitals.

Information has long served as a proxy for many intangible capitals, from click-through metrics to AdWords prices. To substantiate the intangible capitals exchanged in an ecosystem, information about the exchanges can be collected to represent the capitals themselves. For example, the count of click-throughs represents the traffic through a site, substantiating the advertising service value provided so that financial capital can be reciprocated by the advertiser.

Blogs has increasingly been popular to attract eyeballs that get turned into advertising revenue. As such, blogs serves as a platform for the capture of attention capital. At the foundational level, a website (and the Internet as a whole) is able to capture almost all interactions, thus allowing the substantiation and capture of almost all capitals exchanged over it.

Platform for Value Aggregation

What is even more impressive with the digital platform is the ability to aggregate infinitesimal amounts of capital exchanged into a substantive reservoir of capital that can be transformed to other types of capitals such as financial capital. This is possible because of the almost costless logging of every click or tap for perfect capture of every interaction. Thus, large numbers are not a problem, but an advantage. One is then freed from constraints that come with volume and can focus on increasing the span of one's ecosystem as much as possible.

Achieving Value Transformation

To transform from one capital to another requires an understanding of the transformation factor and the transformation threshold. A single click-through on a website cannot be converted into dollars because the amount of money that a click-through is worth is infinitesimal. Understanding transformation thresholds and the transformation factors allows a business to better gauge the amounts of capitals needed for exchange within its ecosystem, and this understanding is critical to the assessment of sustainability.

Transition is Still Key

To effect transitions from one state of a capital ecosystem to another, a catalyst is usually needed. This catalyst can be very effective if the proposed target state of the transition is desired by the participants involved, that is, if they see net capital gain for themselves in this state. Thus a target transition state should encapsulate net capital gains for the participants involved. The catalyst then has only to initiate the capital movement or movements that likely results in reciprocal movements of capitals in the capital exchanges. For instance, by offering discounts or free shipping at a certain minimum order amount, a merchant triggers purchases of additional related items.

Sustainability is Still the Goal

Transitions to desired states, no matter how designed and achieved, still exist to serve the goal of sustainability of the capital ecosystem. Thus every proposed and realized transition must be tested within the ecosystem for sustainability. Multiple planned transitions and catalysts can be tested together to assess sustainability. The goals of strategies that we discussed in Chapter 6 are to achieve transitions that result in sustainability and optimality for the ecosystem. Thus strategies are no more than a collection of aligned, integrated catalysts that move the ecosystems through intended transitions. As such, strategy sets are larger collections of catalysts where some catalysts are grouped into specific strategies for better conceptualization.

Looking at strategies in this manner, we can see that there will be instances where a catalyst does not achieve the desired transition and the strategy would break down. By addressing the strategy as a collection of catalysts, a re-enactment of the catalyst or its enhanced version can always be implemented. To this end, a capital ecosystem is always adjusting, enhancing, and dynamically catalyzed, true to the nature of a business that is constantly experimenting to tune in with participants' needs and goals, ultimately arriving at the best set of value exchanges for each ecosystem.

"Adults are always asking little
kids what they want to be
when they grow up because
they're looking for ideas."

-Paula Poundstone

10. A Few Ideas

One of the key advantages in utilizing the capital ecosystem framework in examining business networks is the opportunity to recognize the numerous opportunities for capital exchanges currently not taking place in many networks. These capital exchanges directly point to potential business niches or even whole new markets. Capital exchanges powerfully reflect needs of participants through reciprocal capital flows.

In this chapter, we recall the power of the framework by highlighting some ideas just through our examination of certain markets and their capital ecosystems. Michael Porter's oft-quoted *Competitive Advantage* examines the make-up of an industry through the consideration of the five forces as well as the value chains that are key to the delivery of products and services.   The resource-based view (RBV) advanced by Barney expands the focus to the capabilities of a firm in terms of its valuable, rare, imperfectly imitable, and non-substitutable resources.[79]   Iansiti and Levien advanced the "ecosystem strategy" that Moore conceptualized in 1993 to encourage a paradigm shift toward envisioning businesses as sets of highly connected and interdependent participants.[80]   Our framework extends the "ecosystem strategy" concept with a refinement of the value creation and capture processes via the constructs of the capital taxonomy and capital ecosystem.   It also incorporates the advancement of "value network" concepts championed by Verna Allee[81], the business value modeling insights by Japp Gordign[82], and the work of Alexander Osterwalder and Yves Pigneur[83] in the realm of business model design.   Our framework focuses on the formalization and quantification of value flows among firms and individuals, as well as within firms, in the forms of capitals that are reciprocally exchanged. This is done to recognize and develop

---

[79] **Barney, Jay.** *Firm Resources and Sustainable Competitive Advantage.* New York : s.n., 1991.

[80] **Iansiti, Marco and Levien, Roy.** *The Keystone Advantage: What the New Dynamics of Business Ecosystems Mean for Strategy, Innovation, and Sustainability.* Boston : Harvard Business School Publishing, 2004.

[81] *Value Network Analysis and Value Conversion of Tangible and Intangible Assets.* **Allee.** s.l. : Emerald Insights, 2008. Journal of Intellectual Capital. pp. 5-24.

[82] **Gordijn, Jaap.** e3value. *e3value.* [Online] 2011. http://www.e3value.com/index.php.

[83] *An e-Business Model Ontology for Modeling e-Business.* **Osterwalder, Alexander and Pigneur, Yves.** Bled, Slovenia : s.n., 2002. 15th Bled Electronic Commerce Conference.

innovative, high-value, and sustainable businesses. This conceptualization, at the most superficial level, allows us to better recognize the many forces that moderate economic exchanges in a market. At the deeper level, it helps us anticipate the consequences, the transitions, the states, and the sustainability of the network through the accounting of different types of capitals, tangible and intangible.

Rather than examining only those capitals that are tangible or well-known, the digital entrepreneur should expand his sphere of consideration to capitals that have material effect on the ecosystem even when they are not recognized and captured. The greatest entrepreneurs see opportunities of which the existing market is completely unaware or dismisses as unimportant. Better yet, they recognize the forces that underlie these opportunities. They then validate their ideas by examining the forces and connecting their conceptualization with existing developments via hypotheses and experiments.

These are interesting times. The power of the connected economy has been felt in every aspect of our lives, from the millions of Likes a company receives on Facebook to the Obama presidential campaign garnering an unheard-of amount of campaign contributions from millions of individuals.[84] Riding the wave of social networking, many opportunities exist for companies that provide tools for transitions to states of more connections and higher density. Companies such as CloudSponge focus specifically on delivering more connections both from participants already in an ecosystem and those not yet a part of it. LinkedIn provides a ready and steady supply of members and connections for over 100 million professionals. Even more tremendous opportunities exist in capturing and channeling information and social capitals. Investments and traction achieved by companies like Klout, GetSatisfaction, and GetGlue point to the validity and significance of intangible capitals and the need to capture and aggregate them for transformation.

Mobile devices and location-based services (LBS) move the access of the digital platform directly to the consumer 24 hours a day, enabling additional opportunities for interactions and value exchanges. These developments create a wide array of opportunities for additional capital capture, aggregation, and transformation. Now, more than ever, because of the numerous intangible capitals being captured and the transformations that have emerged, the need to coordinate and aggregate the capital exchanges is critical. Digital

[84] **Schifferes, Steve.** Internet key to Obama victories. *BBC News.* June 12, 2008.

entrepreneurs should strive for a comprehensive recognition of all capitals exchanged within the capital ecosystem, arming themselves with the tools to identify capital exchange gaps that represent untapped business opportunities, whether in a new or mature market.

Chapter

11

> "As for the future, your task is
> not to foresee it, but to enable
> it."
>
> -Antoine de Saint-Exupery

11. To Come...

L et us look forward to a very near future where all
capitals are recognized, efficiently utilized, and
exchanged to unlock tremendous wealth, while
bringing about the highest levels of satisfaction for consumers.
This volume has succeeded if it has competently called
attention to the enormous opportunities that await all
entrepreneurs in the digital domain. Not only will they capture
their piece of prosperity from the digital wealth machine, but
also gain satisfaction with the knowledge that true values are
created with each and every type of capitals catalyzed and
exchanged.

Bibliography

U.S v. Microsoft: Court's Findings of Fact, 98-1232 (THE UNITED STATES DISTRICT COURT FOR THE DISTRICT OF COLUMBIA November 5, 1999).

7-Eleven, I. (2011, April). *History.* Retrieved from 7-Eleven Corporate: http://corp.7-eleven.com

Acquia. (2011). *Acquia - About Us.* Retrieved May 31, 2011, from Acquia is Drupal made Simple | Acquia: http://acquia.com/about-us

AICPA. (2005). *EBRC.* Retrieved from AICPA: http://www.aicpa.org/InterestAreas/AccountingAndAuditing/Resourc es/EBR/Pages/EnhancedBusinessReportingConsortium.aspx

Allee, V. (2008). Value Network Analysis and Value Conversion of Tangible and Intangible Assets. *Journal of Intellectual Capital* (pp. 5-24). Emerald Insights.

Anderson, C. (2006). *The Long Tail: Why the Future of Business is Selling Less of More.* New York: Hyperion.

Anthony, S. D., & Gilbert , C. G. (2006, Spring). Can the Newspaper Industry Stare Disruption in the Face? *Nieman Reports.*

Asharya, K. (2011, January 19). *Netflix Moves Towards Streaming-Only Services.* Retrieved May 31, 2011, from ITVedia: http://www.itvedia.com/news/1047.html

Barney, J. (1991). *Firm Resources and Sustainable Competitive Advantage.* New York.

Brandenburger, A. M., & Nalebuff, B. J. (1996). *Co-Opetition.* New York: Currency Doubleday.

Brown, S. (2011, June 8). *How GSA Schedule takes your Brand Name Ahead .* Retrieved June 10, 2011, from Amazines: http://www.amazines.com/article_detail.cfm?articleid=2944565

Bureau, T. B. (2011, May 25). *ISO 9001 proven to help win new business .* Retrieved May 31, 2011, from The British Assessment Bureau: http://www.british-assessment.co.uk/news-story.asp?newsTitle=ISO-9001-proven-to-help-win-new-business-

Chaffey, D., Ellis-Chadwick, F., Mayer, R., & Johnston, K. (2009). *Internet Marketing: Strategy, Implementation, Practice.* Essex: Pearson Education Limited.

Charles, D. (2006). GPS Is Smartening Up Your Cell Phone. *NPR.*

Christensen, C. M. (1997). *The Innovator's Dilemma: The Revolutionary Book that Will Change the Way You Do Business.* New York: HarperCollins Publishers.

ConstantContact. (2011, May 31). *Email Marketing Overview - Constant Contact.* Retrieved May 31, 2011, from Constant Contact: http://www.constantcontact.com/email-marketing/index.jsp

Dahlen, C. (2010, November). *Observations on Groupon Business Model - a Primer.* Retrieved May 31, 2011, from Slideshare: http://www.slideshare.net/dahlenc/groupon-business-model

Davidow, W. H., & Malone, M. S. (1992). *The Virtual Corporation*. New York: Harper Business.

Davis, D. (2011, March 29). Amazon offers free online storage and streaming of music and video. *Internet Retailer*.

DIRECTV. (2011, May 31). *DIRECTV: Refer a Friend*. Retrieved May 31, 2011, from DIRECTV: http://www.directv.com/DTVAPP/referral/referralProgram.jsp

Economist, t. (2010, September 2). Putting your money where your mouse is. *The Economist*.

Edvinsson, L. (1997). Developing intellectual capital at Skandia. *Long Range Planning, 30*(3), 363-373.

Farber, D. (2011, May 3). *Latest Facebook Investment Values Company at $65 Billion - CNBC*. Retrieved May 31, 2011, from CNBC: http://www.cnbc.com/id/41892971/Latest_Facebook_Investment_Val ues_Company_at_65_Billion

Forum for the Future. (2010). *The Five Capitals model*. Retrieved from Forum for the Future: http://www.forumforthefuture.org/projects/the-five-capitals

Gladwell, M. (2002). *The Tipping Point: How Little Things Can Make....* Back Bay Books.

Google, I. (2011, May 10). *Summary of Google, Inc. - Yahoo! Finance*. Retrieved from Yahoo! Finance: http://biz.yahoo.com/e/110510/goog10-q.html

Gordijn, J. (2011). *e3value*. Retrieved April 2011, from e3value: http://www.e3value.com/index.php

Hafner, K. (2007, June 18). Restaurant Reservations Go Online . *New York Times*.

Hau, L. (2006, December 11). Newspaper Killer. *Forbes Magazine*.

Howe, J. (2006, June). The Rise of Crowdsourcing . *Wired*.

Hsieh, T. (2010). *Delivering Happiness: A Path to Profits, Passion, and Purpose*. New York: Business Plus.

Iansiti, M., & Levien, R. (2004). *The Keystone Advantage: What the New Dynamics of Business Ecosystems Mean for Strategy, Innovation, and Sustainability*. Boston: Harvard Business School Publishing.

IDC. (2011, June 9). *IDC Press Release - prUS22871611*. Retrieved June 9, 2011, from IDC: http://www.idc.com/getdoc.jsp?containerId=prUS22871611

InCaS. (2010). *InCaS*. Retrieved from InCaS: http://www.incas-europe.org/index-en.htm

Kelly, K. (2011, 06 13). *Facebook IPO Valuation Could Top $100 Billion: Sources*. Retrieved from CNBC: http://www.cnbc.com/id/43378490

Malik, O. (2011, June 9). *Google +1, Facebook Likes & the Web Commerce Battle*. Retrieved June 9, 2011, from Gigaom: http://gigaom.com/2011/06/02/google-1-vs-facebook-likes/

Mannes, T. (2011, April 22). Union-Tribune's Daily Deal hits big mark. *San Diego Union-Tribune*.

Marmer, M., Herrmann, B. L., & Berman, R. (2011, May 28). *Startup Genome Report*. Retrieved May 31, 2011, from Blackbox: http://startupgenome.cc/pages/startup-genome-report-1

McMillan, L. G. (2002). *Options as a Strategic Investment*. New York: Penguin Putnam.

Moore, J. F. (1993, May/June). Predators and Prey: A New Ecology of Competition. *Harvard Business Review*.

Nobelprize.org. (2001, October 10). *The Prize in Economics 2001 - Press Release*. Retrieved May 31, 2011, from Nobelprize.org: http://nobelprize.org/nobel_prizes/economics/laureates/2001/press.html

Osterwalder, A., & Pigneur, Y. (2002). An e-Business Model Ontology for Modeling e-Business. *15th Bled Electronic Commerce Conference*. Bled, Slovenia.

Penenberg, A. (2009). *Viral Loop*. New York: Hyperion.

Porter, M. (1980). *Competitive Advantage*. Boston.

Press, A. (2011, May 3). Sony says 25 million more accounts hacked. *USA Today*, p. 1.

Relations, Y. M. (2005). *The History of Yahoo! - How It All Started...* Retrieved May 31, 2011, from Yahoo Media Relations Home: http://docs.yahoo.com/info/misc/history.html

Reuters. (2011). Thousands of Citi customers at risk after hacker attack. *Thompson Reuters*.

Ries, E. (2011). *The Lean Startup*. New York: Crown Business.

Roediger, U. (2009, August 17). *How Oracle BPA Suite and generic ARIS Platform products play together*. Retrieved May 31, 2011, from ARIS Community: http://www.ariscommunity.com/print/users/uro/2009-08-17-how-oracle-bpa-suite-and-generic-aris-platform-products-play-together

Salesforce.com. (2011, April). *Force.com*. Retrieved from Salesforce.com: http://www.salesforce.com/platform/

Salter, C. (2007, September 1). Girl Power. *Fast Company*.

Schifferes, S. (2008, June 12). Internet key to Obama victories. *BBC News*.

Scratchback. (2011). *Scratchback FAQ's*. Retrieved from Scratchback: http://www.scratchback.com/

Shapiro, C., & Varian, H. (1999). *Information Rules: A Strategic Guide to the Network Economy*. Boston: HBS Press.

Shuen, A. (2008). *Web 2.0: A Strategy Guide*. Sebastopol: O'Reilly Media.

Steiner, C. (2010, August 30). Meet The Fastest Growing Company Ever. *Forbes Magazine*, p. 3.

Story, L., & Helft, M. (2007, April 14). Google Buys DoubleClick for $3.1 Billion. *The New York Times*.

Stross, R. (2008, January 13). From 10 Hours a Week, $10 Million a Year . *The New York Times*.

Surowiecki, J. (2010, December 20). Groupon Clipping. *The New Yorker*.

TechCrunch. (2010, October 15). *Mojopages - Crunchbase Profile*. Retrieved May 31, 2011, from Crunchbase:
http://www.crunchbase.com/company/mojopages

TechCrunch. (2011, May 29). *Klout - Crunchbase Profile*. Retrieved May 31, 2011, from Crunchbase: http://www.crunchbase.com/company/klout

Tony, H., Hanny, T., Lund, B., & Scott, J. (2005, April). Social Bookmarking Tools (I): A General Overview. *D-Lib Magazine*.

Warren, C. (2011, January 17). *A Guide to Kickstarter & Crowd Funding [INFOGRAPHIC]*. Retrieved May 31, 2011, from Mashable: http://mashable.com/2011/01/17/kickstarter-crowd-funding-infographic/

White, A. L. (2010). The Five Capitals of Integrated Reporting: Toward a Holistic Architecture for Corporate Disclosure. Boston: Harvard Business School.

WICI. (2007). *WICI*. Retrieved from WICI: http://www.wici-global.com/

Wikipedia. (2011, May 4). *Amazon Web Services - Wikipedia*. Retrieved May 31, 2011, from Wikipedia:
http://en.wikipedia.org/wiki/Amazon_Web_Services

Wikipedia. (2011, May 25). *foursquare (social network) - Wikipedia*. Retrieved May 31, 2011, from Wikipedia:
http://en.wikipedia.org/wiki/Foursquare_(social_network)

Wikipedia. (2011, June 11). *iTunes Store - Wikipedia*. Retrieved June 11, 2011, from Wikipedia: http://en.wikipedia.org/wiki/ITunes_Store

Wikipedia. (2011, May 31). *Virtual Office - Wikipedia*. Retrieved May 31, 2011, from Wikipedia: http://en.wikipedia.org/wiki/Virtual_office

Wikipedia. (2011, May 7). *Wikipedia*. Retrieved May 31, 2011, from Wikipedia: http://en.wikipedia.org/wiki/Threadless

Wire, B. (2009). Zynga's FarmVille Becomes Largest and Fastest Growing Social Game Ever. Business Wire.

Xignite. (2010, June 22). *NASDAQ and Xignite to Provide On-Demand Tick Data via Cloud Computing Platform: Xignite Press*. Retrieved May 31, 2011, from Xignite:
http://www.xignite.com/News/PressRelease.aspx?articleid=215

Xignite. (2011, April 26). *NASDAQ'S "Big Data" Cloud Service Launches on Xignite's Platform*. Retrieved May 31, 2011, from Xignite: http://www.xignite.com/News/PressRelease.aspx?articleid=248

Zakon, R. H. (2010, December 15). *Hobbes' Internet Timeline 10.1*. Retrieved May 31, 2011, from Hobbes' Internet Timeline: http://www.zakon.org/robert/internet/timeline/

Glossary

access strategies – Strategies that leverage the demand for getting to the internet via dial-up and corporate and university research networks.

advertising strategies - Strategies based on the viability of the business model in which banner advertising alone can completely support the costs of a digital business. The most well-known example is PlentyOfFish.

analytics strategies – Strategies built upon the recognition that statistical reporting and calculations are a crucial component of business and for competitive capabilities.

augmented reality strategies – Strategies that are based on mash-up strategies, deriving their power from the superimposition of digital information onto information about physical reality. An example is the physical map photography or video that is overlaid with street information and relevant advertising.

bandwidth strategies – Strategies based on the recognition that demand for internet usage had quickly snowballed and increase in bandwidth and internet capacity was considered most critical.

business ecosystem - A network of businesses in which the businesses are inter-dependent on each other for exchanges of values and capitals that provide viable business transactions for each of them individually.

community strategies - Strategies based on the creation online groups that gather and collaborate in a closed environment to share resources, knowledge, expertise, while forming and observing group norms and protocols, with the help of administrator(s) or mediator(s).

connection - A representation of the mutual recognition and contact between two nodes in a network.

crowdfunding strategies- Strategies based on the application of crowdsourcing to raise money, or funding, gathering small amounts of funds from many sources to raise a large amount.

crowdsourcing strategies – Strategies that leverage the power of the masses and the "wisdom of crowd".

density - The number of connections among the nodes and groups of nodes within a network.

games strategies – Strategies that leverage the engagement and traction of games. Gamification of websites have been proven to creative significant results in the level of engagement and stickiness.

infrastructure strategies – Strategies that take advantage of the increased importance of providing infrastructure underlying and enabling internet usage.

intermediary strategies – Strategies that based on the ability of middle-man services to effect transactions, ranging from infomediaries to exchanges and dating services.

internet services strategies – Strategies based on the creation of services on the internet that replaced or improve those in the physical world. These range from on-line trading to on-line shopping and on-line book-selling.

internetworking strategies - Refers to strategies that leverage the connections of evermore numerous and far-flung networks of computers.

location-based services strategies - Strategies that rely on the geo-spotting capability of mobile devices to supply services that are relevant and convenient to the user.

long tail strategies – Strategies based on the recognition of the internet's capability to sell to many small groups of customers desiring uncommon feature sets.

mash-ups strategies - Strategies that derive their power from the combination and juxtaposition of two or more sets of information from different dimensions or types of measurement.

mobile strategies – Strategies that leverage the advent of smart phones, which allows mobile access to the internet and the capabilities of location-based services.

n-sided market - A market in which there are more than two groups of buyers, sellers, partners, and third parties exchanging different types of goods, services, and capitals.

platform strategies – Strategies based on the formalization and encapsulation of common internet services into a set of customized capabilities that consuming businesses can leverage Examples include the provision of API's and customization capabilities by Facebook, Amazon, and SalesForce.com.

plumbing strategies – Strategies based on the provisioning of infrastructure software and hardware that enable the increase in internet bandwidth.

social bookmarking strategies – Strategies that leverage the popularity of services that enabling the marking of internet destinations and content, as well as the ability to share those markings among one's social networks.

social network strategies – Strategies based on the creation and growth of large networks of connected individuals. Examples of hugely successful and well-known social networks include FaceBook, LinkedIn, Meetup, and Bebo.

span - The expanse of a network, including the number of nodes and the distances between those nodes.

strategy lineage - A string of strategies that are logically and synergistically connected to each other, reinforcing the advantages of each strategy, while neutralizing its short-comings.

strategy set - The set of strategies that are relevant to a business or an ecosystem. The strategy set is not necessary a strategy lineage. Once the strategies within the set are suitably aligned, a strategy lineage can be evolved to provide strategy leverage, reinforcement, and defensive positioning.

user access tools strategies – Strategies based on the recognition that tools to access the internet are critical to internet usage and the ability to capture digital scale and.

value aggregation - The act of accumulating capitals in any and all forms within a network.

value alignment - A process by which values created within a business ecosystem are leveraged and supported by the activities in that network, instead of opposed or conflicted.

value capture - The act of gathering capital in any and all forms (e.g., information capital, reputation capital).

value exchanges - The transactions that occur among nodes in a network involving units of capitals such as financial capital, intellectual capital, or tangible manufactured capital.

value transformation efficiency - The degree to which capital of one kind is transformed to another with relatively high results.

value transformation - The act of converting one type of capital to another, e.g., information capital to financial capital, as a representation of monetizing analytics data.

viral strategies - Strategies based on the massive spreading of messages and the exponentially fast and far spreading of information across networks of individuals for ideas that not only capture the attention of the receiver, but also compels him or her to continue its propagation.

Index

About the Author

Stefan Nguyen is Founder and CEO of Next Ignite, an innovation accelerator focused solely on digital companies. He is also serving as Chief Strategy Officer of Chroniclr™, a path-breaking social media platform. Prior to Next Ignite, Stefan was Co-Founder and Chief Technical Officer of Xignite, the leading cloud services provider of on-demand financial market data and award-winning on-demand data distribution solutions. Stefan was also one of the original developers of the popular Oracle® E-Business suite of products used by most Fortune 1000 companies and thousands of other enterprises.

Stefan has an MBA from Columbia Business School, where he studied under Nobel laureate Joseph Stiglitz. Stefan received his BS in Electrical Engineering from Northwestern University.

www.ingramcontent.com/pod-product-compliance
Lightning Source LLC
Chambersburg PA
CBHW072351200326
41519CB00015B/3732